READING POVERTY IN AMERICA

In this book Shannon's major premise remains the same as the 1998 edition titled *Reading Poverty:* Poverty has everything to do with American public schooling—how it is theorized, how it is organized, and how it runs. Competing ideological representations of poverty underlie school assumptions about intelligence, character, textbook content, lesson formats, national standards, standardized achievement tests, and business/school partnerships and frame our considerations of each. In this new edition Shannon describes and analyzes the persistence and variation among these expressions of the putative relationships between poverty and reading.

Reaching back to the original ESEA, he provides an update of the ideological struggles to name and respond to poverty through the design, content, and pedagogy of reading education, showing how, through their representations and framing, advocates of liberal, conservative, and neoliberal interpretations attempt the ideological practice of teaching the public who they are, what they should know, and what they should value about equality, civic society, and reading.

By comparing and contrasting these attempts, teachers and other readers can develop new understandings of reading education policies and use their new knowledge to decide whether or not to accept the positions offered through these different iterations. For those who decline these offers, Shannon presents examples of radical democratic interpretations of the relationship between poverty and reading education that offer the poor, the public, students, and teachers positions as agents in redistribution of economic, cultural and political capital in the United States. Through these steps, he demonstrates the double entendre of the title—to read how poverty is rhetorically as well as materially produced in the United States and to recognize an enriched potential for reading and education in the lives of the poor and public life.

Patrick Shannon is Professor of Education, Pennsylvania State University, USA. He is an elected member of the Reading Hall of Fame.

READING POVERTY IN AMERICA

Patrick Shannon

NEW YORK AND LONDON

First published 2014
by Routledge
711 Third Avenue, New York, NY 10017

and by Routledge
2 Park Square, Milton Park, Abingdon, Oxon OX14 4RN

Routledge is an imprint of the Taylor & Francis Group, an informa business

© 2014 Taylor & Francis

The right of the Author to be identified as author of this work has been asserted by him in accordance with sections 77 and 78 of the Copyright, Designs and Patents Act 1988.

All rights reserved. No part of this book may be reprinted or reproduced or utilized in any form or by any electronic, mechanical, or other means, now known or hereafter invented, including photocopying and recording, or in any information storage or retrieval system, without permission in writing from the publishers.

Trademark notice: Product or corporate names may be trademarks or registered trademarks, and are used only for identification and explanation without intent to infringe.

Library of Congress Cataloging-in-Publication Data

Shannon, Patrick, 1951–
 Reading poverty in America / Patrick Shannon.
   pages cm
 Includes bibliographical references and index.
 1. Poor—Education—Social aspects—United States. 2. Reading—Social aspects—United States. 3. Literacy—Political aspects—United States. 4. Poverty—United States. I. Title.
   LC4086.S53 2014
   82371.826′94—dc23
   2013040556

ISBN: 978-0-415-72272-8 (hbk)
ISBN: 978-0-415-72273-5 (pbk)
ISBN: 978-1-315-85812-8 (ebk)

Typeset in Bembo
by Apex CoVantage, LLC

Printed and bound in the United States of America by Publishers Graphics, LLC on sustainably sourced paper.

CONTENTS

Preface		*vii*
1	Poverty: A National Disgrace	1
2	Conditions and Consequences	9
3	Opportunity: Liberals	31
4	Character: Conservatives	55
5	Competition: Neoliberals	79
6	Collective Agency: Radical Democrats	101
References		*123*
Index		*137*

PREFACE

We are rapidly approaching the 50th anniversary of the Elementary and Secondary Education Act (ESEA) of 1965. In the wake of Michael Harrington's *The Other America* (1962) and Walter Heller's (1964) *Annual Report of the Council of Economic Advisors*, the Johnson Administration made the original Act part of the War on Poverty. At that time, one in four American children were considered poor. Lest we forget the Johnson Administration's faith in education, Commissioner of Education Francis Keppel (1965) remarked at the signing of the original ESEA, "Archimedes told us many centuries ago: 'Give me a lever long enough and supported strongly enough and I can move the world.' Today, at last, we have the prospect of a lever long enough and supported strongly enough to do something for our children of poverty. The lever is education, and the fulcrum is federal assistance." Title 1 of the ESEA funded special programs, teachers, and tests for low-income children who were deemed to be behind in learning to read. In a sense, then, teachers of reading were to supply some of the muscle to move the world for America's poor.

Today, U.S. poverty rates exceed those of 1965, although the percentage of children living in poverty has dropped modestly to 22. Charles Murray's *Coming Apart* (2012) captures the media attention about poverty, and Paul Ryan's "Path to Prosperity" budget proposal is the talk of both chambers of the federal legislature. The latest iteration of the ESEA, No Child Left Behind, expired in 2007, but by law it remains active until a formal reauthorization of the Act is considered. In his 2010 State of the Union Address, President Obama echoed Keppel's sentiment: "In the 21st century, the best antipoverty program around is a first class education." Yet his enthusiasm for the potential of education is compromised by concerns about the outcomes of public schooling, because on average American students score below other nations on international tests of reading (as well as math and science).

"We have to get better faster than ever before at education" suggests Secretary of Education Arne Duncan (2011) or we will lose our international economic status and jeopardize our national security (Council on Foreign Relations, 2012). To accelerate those improvements, the Obama Administration advocates for common core standards across the nation and teacher evaluation schemes tied to student outcomes on standardized reading tests. In this way, current schooling and teacher practices are cast as impediments to individual and national prosperity.

As teachers and citizens, what are we to make of these similarities and differences? Poverty remains; it even grows. Education is still considered the lever. The federal government's war on poverty has ended, however, and schools have been positioned as the only tool and teachers the only muscle to move all students up economically, to save the middle class, and to retain the United States' position in the world. Reading the similarities between 1965 and now keeps us talking and working with all interested parties in order to learn what "coming apart," "paths to prosperity," and "antipoverty" could mean today, and how they could be connected to deep American commitments to equal opportunities in life ("all created equal . . .").

Such reading will make us more socially competent as taxpayers, citizens, and teachers, casting us as agents within others' plans for the future. Reading the differences, however, enables us to see that alternative futures were promised in the past and are being promised now. Those distinct futures afford different positions to one and all—we can recognize what is before us and imagine how it might be otherwise. By pushing past the similarities in order to consider what the differences might mean, we transform our reading from consumption of what others offer us to the production of ourselves as agents of and in the work of education. We make as well as choose our positions because we are not simply the muscle, but also the imagination behind that lever.

First Things First

If you look at those international test scores carefully, then the government's official rationale and direction of school reform become problematic. When Berliner (2009), Bracey (2009), and Krashen, Lee, and McQuillan (2010) disaggregated American test scores on the 2006 Progress in International Reading Literacy Study (PIRLS), each found that poverty accounted for the gap in scores between American students and students from high-scoring countries. Students from American schools with few students eligible for free or reduced lunch (a measure of at least middle income) scored as high or higher than students from the highest-scoring countries, and students from schools with many students eligible (a measure of low income) scored among students from the lowest-performing countries. Each concluded that America has a two-tiered public school system— one for the middle and upper classes and one for low-income students. Reardon

(2011) demonstrated that this gap in performance on reading tests between economic classes has grown by 40 percent since 1970.

Yet, Rowan (2011) marshaled compelling evidence that carefully designed programs can improve low-income children's reading test scores modestly, but significantly. Often these improvements require that entire schools attend to five essential supports: professional capacity of teachers and administrators; focused school learning climate; strong parent, school, and community ties; clear and aligned instructional guidelines; and supportive leadership (Bryk, Sebring, Allensworth, Luppescu, & Easton, 2010). However, Bryk and others found improvements rarely took hold in schools that served the truly disadvantaged, "where palpable human needs walk through the door virtually every day" (p. 196). That is, even these essential in-school interventions were not enough to overcome the effects of poverty on these students (Bryk et al. estimate over 40,000 in Chicago schools alone). In order to help these students gain equal opportunities to learn to read, they hypothesized that outside-of-school interventions would be needed as well.

Different levels of government do provide outside-of-school supports for income (earned income tax credits, unemployment insurance, and temporary assistance for needy families), health care (Medicare, prescription drug programs, and Medicaid), hunger (Supplemental Nutrition Assistance Program, school lunches, and emergency food assistance), and housing (public housing assistance). Without these programs, many more American children would be classified as truly disadvantaged and their lives would be much more difficult (Edelman, 2012). However, current interventions are insufficient to meet the basic human needs of the truly disadvantaged. For example, 50 percent of families currently below the poverty line report food insecurity monthly (Nord & Parker, 2010). Forty-four million Americans are not covered by health insurance and are less likely to seek medical treatment when needed (Kaiser Family State Health Facts, 2012). Only 20 percent of eligible families receive federal housing assistance (Acs & Turner, 2008). And direct income support for the poor requires opportunities for employment, making it unavailable to many when the unemployment rate hovers at 8 percent nationally and reaches as high as 40 percent in urban and rural areas. Hungry, sick, sleepy, and anxious students have fewer opportunities of learning to read at school.

For these reasons, teachers should be reading poverty through current in-school and out-of-school interventions. While our knowledge of in-school interventions seems to be headed in a positive direction (Au, 2011),

> the Reagan era changes to social policy—particularly changes in housing policies, income-support policies, and other social safety nets for low-income families—have made life much more difficult for low-income families. Not only do the poor have less money than they did before, they may have fewer social supports as well. (Reardon, 2011, p.110)

Moreover, the arguments promoted in *Coming Apart* and "Path to Prosperity" seek further cutbacks in funding for government assistance programs. The consequences of this direction in policies could be felt in the bodies and minds of low-income children, severely limiting the possibilities of teachers to provide "the best antipoverty program" in the 21st century.

Despite Song and Miskel's (2005) discouraging findings that teachers' professional organizations such as the International Reading Association and the National Council of Teachers of English have little influence over federal reading education policy, teachers cannot accept the position to work harder only in schools while leaving out-of-school matters to politicians, business leaders, and pundits. To do so would be to limit the historic mission of public schools to leverage all students upward economically (Goldin & Katz, 2008) and to prepare all to remake democracy in each generation (Dewey, 1916). We must read poverty to imagine how that mission can be renewed and extended.

> Education without social action is a one-sided value because it has no true power potential. Social action without education is a weak expression of pure energy. Deeds uninformed by educated thought can take false directions. When we go into action and confront our adversaries, we must be as armed with knowledge as they. Our policies should have the strength of deep analysis beneath them to be able to challenge the clever sophistries of our opponents. (King, Jr., 1967, p. 155)

Reading Poverty in America

When I wrote *Reading Poverty* during the fall of 1997, President Clinton had just been reelected. Having ended "welfare as we know it" in 1996, he set his sights on the repeal of the Glass–Steagall Act (1933) and the reauthorization of ESEA during his new term. Permitting commercial banks to engage in securities sales would fuel the financial growth needed to compensate for the decline in American manufacturing and the loss of middle-class jobs and incomes, and ESEA would spread the new skills required in the global innovation economy more evenly among Americans. Clinton targeted reading as primary among those skills. "We know that unless we can read, we will not be able to take advantage of the future or understand the past." At that time, the federal government enjoyed a budget surplus, but 15.1 percent of all Americans and 22.7 percent of children and adolescents lived below the official poverty line.

As I started to rewrite *Reading Poverty,* President Obama had just been reelected. Having expanded private health insurance to near-universal levels in 2010, he seeks to allow parts of the Jobs and Growth Tax Relief Reconciliation Act (2003) to lapse and to reauthorize the ESEA (now five years overdue) during his second term. Permitting the Bush tax cuts to expire for the wealthy (along with spending cuts to entitlement programs) will provide additional revenue to reduce the federal budget deficit exacerbated by the Great Recession, and the new ESEA will ensure all Americans will be competitive workers in the world economy. During his first term, Obama worked to nationalize a world-class reading education system: "I want to commend all of you for acting collectively through the National Governors Association to develop common academic standards [in English language, arts, and math] that will better position our students for success." In 2012, 15.2 percent of American citizens were officially poor, 50 percent of American jobs paid less than $34,000, and 22 percent of children lived below the poverty line.

Although American poverty was rarely mentioned publicly during the 2012 presidential campaign, the concept was at the center of most debates. Having chosen Tea Party leader Representative Paul Ryan as his running mate, Governor Romney argued that his administration would reduce the role of government in the lives of citizens by cutting federal funding for New Deal and War on Poverty programs because they have created a culture of dependency among those receiving aid:

> 47 percent . . . who are dependent upon government, who believe that they are victims, who believe the government has a responsibility to care for them, who believe that they are entitled to health care, to food, to housing, to you-name-it. (quoted in *Mother Jones*, 2012)

In Ryan's proposed budget, ESEA would be cut by 20 percent, charging state and local governments to design public/private educational solutions to help individuals make better choices about their lives. According to Ryan, "the best thing . . . is to teach people good discipline, good character" (as quoted in Allen, 2012). Having started his political career at Empower America with William Bennett, "teaching good character" means a reading education based on books of virtue.

In this new volume, I describe and explain the persistence and variation among these expressions of the putative relationships between poverty and reading. Reaching back to the original ESEA, I provide an update of the ideological struggles to name and respond to poverty through the design, content, and pedagogy of reading education. Through their representations and framing, advocates of liberal, conservative, and neoliberal interpretations attempt the ideological practice of teaching the public who they are, what they should know, and what they should value about equality, civic society, and reading. They invite the public to assume social roles accordingly, to enact their plans competently, and to enjoy the expected consequences with gratitude. By comparing and contrasting these liberal, conservative, and neoliberal attempts, however, teachers and other readers can develop new understandings of reading education policies, of the 40 percent widening in the income achievement gap since 1970, and of student and teacher lives in schools over the past 50 years.

Moreover, readers can use their new knowledge to decide whether they accept the positions offered to the poor, the public, and themselves through these different iterations. For those who decline the offers, I present examples of radical democratic interpretations of the relationship between poverty and reading education that offer the poor, the public, students, and teachers positions as agents in redistribution of economic, cultural, and political capital in the United States. Through these steps, I hope to demonstrate the double entendre of the title—to read how poverty is rhetorically as well as materially produced in the United States and to recognize an enriched potential for reading and education in the lives of the poor and public life. Only the basic premise of the first book will be carried over into this new edition: Poverty has everything to do with American public schooling—how it is theorized, how it is organized, and how it runs. Competing ideological representations of poverty underlie school assumptions about intelligence, character, textbook content, lesson formats, national standards, standardized achievement tests, and business/school partnerships and frame our considerations of each. We can look at the relationships between ideological representations and framing of poverty and the consequent policies, design, and implementation of reading education in order to make decisions about how we wish to live together in and out of schools.

1
POVERTY
A National Disgrace

I Read the News Today, Oh Boy

On the front page of the Sunday Review section of the *New York Times* (December 7, 2012), Nicholas D. Kristof urged Americans to pay more attention to child poverty. He pointed out that America's antipoverty programs—Social Security and Medicare, specifically—have been successful in reducing poverty rates for the elderly from 35 percent in 1959 to 9 percent today, but reported that 22 percent of children remain in poverty. He attributed this difference in outcome to the fact that the elderly have organized and vote regularly, and lamented that children don't have a political voice. Speaking for poor children, he advocated for early intervention programs that will help parents learn to provide their children with oral and written language experiences that science has shown will prepare them to succeed at school and beyond. "There's a time to transform their lives, and they . . . should be a national priority" (Kristof, 2012, p. 9).

Writing under the headline, "Profiting from a Child's Illiteracy," Kristof began this campaign by retelling a story of rural Kentucky parents who withdrew their children from literacy programs because learning to read could make them ineligible for federal financial assistance programs for disabled children. "Many people in hillside mobile homes here are poor and desperate, and a $698 monthly check per child from the Supplemental Security Income [SSI] program goes a long way—and those checks continue until the child turns 18" (Kristof, 2012, p. 1). He explained that the SSI program was originally designed in 1972 to enable a parent to remain at home in order to care for a child with severe physical and/or mental disabilities; over time, the poor have subverted SSI to cover "fuzzier intellectual disabilities." "This is painful for a liberal to admit, but conservatives have a point when they suggest that America's safety net can sometimes entangle people in a soul-crushing dependency" (Kristof, 2012, p. 1).

Kristof offers much to think about in his brief op-ed piece. His topic tugs at our heartstrings. Innocent children live in poverty through no fault of their own, and with appropriate educational attention, their lives could be transformed. We should act accordingly, he pleads, and he has a plan that competes with other solutions for sufficient political power to enact that desired change. To garner our support, he represents poverty for us and frames it, pointing us toward the common sense of his solution. *Reading Poverty* is about this topic, this struggle among alternatives, and this process of reading representations, frames, and ideologies surrounding poverty in America in order to decide on courses of action. And as Kristof implies, the direction of those courses will be set through reading education and political power.

A Good Place to Start

"Profiting from a Child's Illiteracy" provides a useful tool to explain the framework for reading poverty. Kristof assumes that poverty is a national problem. Using statistics and stories, he provides a glimpse of what it means to be poor. Poverty results from a lack of income to be sure, he states, but he implies that it does not necessarily result in discomfort because 8 of 10 poor families enjoy air conditioning, washing machines, and microwave ovens. Poor adults, he explains, are often young, female, and with children. Raped by family members and introduced to narcotics, they weigh their opportunities for income carefully, finding it easier to rely on food stamps and disability payments than to join the army or marry. Recognizing that readers might find his portraits to be more caricatures than characteristic of the poor, Kristof tempers his rhetoric—"this is what poverty sometimes looks like"—and offers two stories of mothers working to provide for their children. One is "equipped with crackling intelligence" and the other, who is pregnant with twins, walks two miles each way to work because her $500 car won't start. Kristof is willing to "bet" on the first one and her son, but he worries "that efforts to help [the second] may end with a mixed record" (Kristof, 2012, p. 9).

In Chapter 2, I present more nuanced descriptions of who is poor in America, the conditions of their poverty, and its effects on infants, children, and adolescents than the one that Kristof offers. Although the official definition of poverty was established in 1963, the determination of who is poor is still hotly contested among social scientists and journalists. In fact, Kristof's employer, the *New York Times*, presents poverty as both an absolute and a relative term and describes a continuum from "extreme" to "official" to "near" levels in which people struggle to sustain their families and themselves. Kristof's "sometimes" poverty in Kentucky differs markedly from other rural areas as well as urban environments and the suburbs—where poverty rates have increased dramatically over the past 20 years.

Behind what Kristof labels "the soul crushing dependence" lie the physiological, social, and spiritual consequences of poverty, which are mediated in complex ways by a tangle of government programs. If we are to act on poverty as Kristof desires, then we must have a clearer picture of what it is and what it does.

Kristof followed Save the Children employees around Kentucky in order to see "a model of what does work" to break the cycle of generational poverty. "Almost anytime the question is poverty, the answer is children" (Kristof, 2012, p. 9), he reports. Save the Children trains community members to visit poor mothers in order to improve their parenting skills—"read to their children, tell stories, talk to them, and hug them." The volunteers demonstrate these skills with the children and lend books and supplies to enable parents to practice the skills between visits. School personnel verified for Kristof that this program has indeed been successful in preparing poor children to begin school on par with their middle-class peers. "I hope that the budget negotiations in Washington may offer us a chance to take money from SSI and invest in early childhood initiatives instead" (Kristof, 2012, p. 9). Across his article, Kristof is clear that poverty is not a natural condition; rather, it is a human artifact that could be remade one child at a time, if the political will existed.

In Chapters 3, 4, and 5 I take up those struggles among political wills that Kristof mentions in his article as advocates argue over the definition, causes, and solutions to American poverty. Similar to Kristof's format and my earlier examples of presidents and a presidential hopeful, each advocate supplies texts that represent and frame poverty according to the ideas, beliefs, and values that hold their group together. For example, Kristof implies that he's a liberal who admits that conservatives aren't always wrong about poverty. In Chapter 3 I flesh out a liberal position on poverty—one that begins with those programs that Kristof acknowledges have been successful in reducing poverty for the elderly. Social Security was devised during the New Deal of the 1930s, and Medicare was born during the War on Poverty of the 1960s. That war offered housing and food security programs as well, which, according to Kristof, have worked to keep the poor comfortable, at least physically. Head Start, a precursor of his Save the Children plan, is a War on Poverty staple as well but, curiously, "liberal" Kristof fails to mention it in his article. All these programs were/are intended to alleviate some problems for the poor, enabling them equal access to opportunities to participate successfully in the economy. In this way, Kristof's call for federal funds to provide proven effective educational interventions could be classified as a liberal act.

Kristof's description of the Kentucky culture of poverty makes a conservative point. Remember President Reagan's description of "welfare queens" from the south side of Chicago, who scammed government programs in order to enjoy tax-free incomes? As I'll explain in Chapter 4, conservatives believe that individuals' bad decisions cause poverty. According to conservatives, poor individuals lack intelligence, follow bad cultural habits, or practice moral relativism, precluding them from using federal programs to gain social mobility. Although Kristof seems unwilling to concede these points completely—"our poverty programs do rescue many people"—he does acknowledge that "other times they backfire" to create dependency among individuals, who congregate together, enabling these debilitating traits to be passed among generations. Axiomatically for conservatives, federal assistance programs encourage these traits and subsequent socialization because the programs provide individuals with alternatives to fending for themselves—accepting whatever work is available, joining the military, staying married, deferring material and emotional gratifications, and attending church. According to conservatives, each of these acts would be a sign of the poor taking responsibility to provide for their families and themselves, making them worthy of charity if and when they needed it. If the Save the Children program were conservative, then it would include decision-making routines for the adults to master and explicit virtuous storylines for both adults and children to imbibe. Kristof doesn't tell us whether these were attributes of the training sessions he observed.

Between these positions lies a neoliberal perspective on poverty. Few people identify as neoliberals. Rather, as I'll explain in Chapter 5, "neoliberal" is a label applied when liberals have lost faith in traditional government-directed solutions to social problems and have adopted more conservative ones. Kristof's rhetoric about the Kentucky culture gave me pause about his claims to liberalism. A liberal, it seems to me, would qualify the sensationalism of the story about parents trading their children's future for an immediate and consistent $700, by explaining why those parents are so "desperate." (And liberal Peter Edelman responded precisely in this way in a letter to the editor of the *New York Times* three days after Kristof's article appeared.) Moreover, a liberal wouldn't miss the opportunity to tout the federal government's Head Start alternative to Save the Children, a nongovernment agency imported from Britain in 1932. Rather than call for full funding for Head Start, Kristof presents a market-based solution in which the federal government would make funding available for which private agencies like Save the Children could compete to provide poor children with the skills necessary for success at school and in the global economy beyond it. Neoliberals believe that people are poor because they do not possess sufficient skills to compete for above-poverty wages. In my mind, then, Kristof offered a neoliberal argument about children in poverty.

Across these three positions, Kristof describes reading education as the basic antipoverty program. Agencies would intervene appropriately in order to provide opportunities to learn, to correct bad personal and cultural choices, or to begin the process of human capital development that comes respectively in the forms of scientifically based best parenting practices, morally virtuous lessons, or world-class knowledge and skills. These seeds in early childhood would be nurtured accordingly through childhood and adolescence with literacy interventions until each individual is ready to enter society with the correct competence to sustain him- or herself, to enter marriage, and, then, to raise families without future possibilities of poverty for any member. And if these respective solutions were funded adequately to reach the 22 percent of American children who live in poverty, then, Kristof implies, and advocates of liberal, conservative, and neoliberal positions promise, poverty could end within one generation. This is their hope for the poor—to fit into established futures.

In Chapter 6, I offer a different approach to poverty in America. Although Kristof mentions that the elderly have been successful because they see themselves, and are recognized, as agents within the political debates about aging, he doesn't seriously entertain that type of solution for the poor. Rather he apes the assumptions of other political advocates, thinking for the poor, speaking for them, and calling on powerful others to find solutions for them. His "reading" intervention is designed to make the poor become socially competent on his terms. This is not how the elderly work as a group; they forced governments and society members to recognize their concerns as legitimate and to redistribute social, economic, and cultural benefits accordingly. Across the 20th century, labor organizations, racial groups, women, and gays have acted similarly, raising their consciousness, organizing, and acting not to fit in according to others' plans, but to change laws, norms, and practices to include their plans for themselves within the swing of American lives.

These groups used their *sociological imaginations*—C. Wright Mills's (1959) term for the ability to understand one's current circumstances as part of larger social/historical conditions and to imagine how those circumstances and conditions could be otherwise. These individuals imagined how the elderly could be recognized as contributors; laborers as creators of profit; and people of color, women, the disabled, and gays as fully human and how society could change to accommodate their imaginations. And then, the individuals found other like-minded people to form coalitions around their issues. They voted, but that was just one of the ways that they sought representation, recognition, and redistribution. They engaged in and continue to engage in discussions, marches, strikes, street theater, organizing, petitions, and letter campaigns, to name a few ways, in order to make space for themselves and others like them in American life. Although coalition members didn't and don't always agree on all issues, they recognize that some specific personal troubles were and are social issues in need of remedies that would be impossible without collective action.

In "Profiting from a Child's Illiteracy" Kristof doesn't just neglect sociological imagination, he denies that it's possible among the poor. He represents them as immoral, irrational, short-sighted, and lazy. He frames the adults as hopeless and the children as salvageable, if the market to fix the children can be made profitable enough for private enterprise. In stark numbers, his solution would "save" 15.7 million children out of the 48.5 million Americans living in poverty—attempts to improve the lives of the 32.8 million adults would be "mixed" and too expensive. I will argue in this book that Kristof is indicative of liberal, conservative, and neoliberal others who wish to speak for the poor in order to do something about poverty. Those individuals cloak their ideologies behind their representations of the poor and frames of poverty in order to teach the public what we should know, who we should be, and what we should value about equality, civic society, and even reading. Their ideologies assure that their solutions are based on the ideas and beliefs that serve to justify and support the interests of their particular group and not the poor, per se. They offer the poor and the public positions in their constellations of America in ways that affirm the relative power of their spots in society. Poverty persists, I'll argue, because power continues to circulate in the same historical ways that create and maintain it.

To fight poverty, then, power relations must change, and radical democratic ideas, beliefs, and values and reading with sociological imagination can be parts of that change. Advocates of radical democracy affirm Americans' individual and collective plurality and resist efforts to separate society into fixed identity groups or paper over difference with calls for the "common good." Rather, they seek to harness the power of that dynamic (differences versus commonalities) in which fluid coalitions form around social issues and work to establish more equitable and inclusive norms. Poverty in the richest country on earth is such a social issue, and the poor, who are made up of members of all those other groups who have been successful in gaining civil rights, are capable of forming effective coalitions and acting. As I argue in Chapter 6, reading with sociological imagination supports these powerful actions by enabling individuals and groups to penetrate the representations and framing of poverty in order to get to the ideologies that position them as powerless and to produce their representations and frames that demand recognition and redistribution of social, cultural, and economic benefits. For radical democrats, the answer is always more democracy.

Ideology, Reading Wide Awake, and More Democracy

Ideology influences our social practices that, in turn, reproduce the ideology. Through institutions (schools, churches, media, clubs, sports, and others), we are to learn the appropriate social practices as "common sense" in order to affirm the ideas, values, and beliefs that are defined as the "common good." That is why different ideological groups compete for control over schooling in general and reading education in particular. Only appropriate content and practices of understanding will ensure the continuation and, perhaps, further development of the groups' interests. Although ideological socialization might work well within close-knit groups that share power—agenda setting, decision making, leadership, and benefits—it works poorly for diverse groups with skewed power relations because, then, the dominant common sense ensures that insiders remain powerful while the marginalized are offered positions to support that power. The United States is a pluralist society with unequal access to political power. Ideologies that do not recognize and embrace that pluralism can only offer us social practices that maintain inequalities.

Liberal, conservative, and neoliberal theories of democracy assume that each citizen possesses a fixed, stable identity and acts rationally and autonomously in his pursuit of self-interest. I use the masculine pronoun because it is important to remember that the original documents of democratic common sense were indeed gendered. "The great and chief end, therefore of men uniting into commonwealths, and putting themselves under government, is the preservation of property" (Locke, 1689/1986, Chapter 9, paragraph 124). According to advocates of these ideologies, the buy-in for democracy is that government provides each citizen equal rights to participate in the identification of norms, rules, and laws intended to promote individual welfare. The government, then, serves as a neutral arbiter when disputes arise in order to maintain the common good. Accordingly, citizens and the government enable and control each other, ensuring both individual freedom and equality of rights as dynamic forces. Just reading Locke's sentence, however, demonstrates that this promise has always been false because not all people were and are recognized as citizens.

Many social groups have had to fight, and continue to fight, to become "citizens" within these democratic theories and governments. Over time, those individuals awoke to recognize that others shared their experiences of personal exclusions. They acknowledged that the ideologies that influenced their every day social practices maintained, and sometimes deepened, those social exclusions across time and space. And they imagined how together they could and should challenge and change those social practices in order to resist exclusion and, then, to become full citizens. With income inequality in America surpassing the levels of its gilded age, with 8 percent unemployment serving as the new normal for "full" employment, and with concerted efforts to prohibit low-income groups from voting, poverty becomes the personal troubles of more and more Americans.

As I will argue, reading is a fundamental social practice of understanding ourselves, our conditions, and our possibilities. I'm not the first to make this argument—even among the individuals I've mentioned in this chapter. President Clinton, President Obama, Governor Romney, Representative Ryan, and editor Kristof place reading at the center of their vision of the common good. However, they worry that high percentages of Americans are illiterate, that our scores on international reading tests suggest that American workers are less productive than their peers in other countries, or that too many Americans read popular culture more than history and good literature. They advocate forms of reading education that will produce their ideals of common sense among all students, teachers, and parents, offering them positions within their versions of the common good.

The ideologies behind those worries and those types of reading education limit our thoughts about reading, narrow the questions we might ask about its possibilities, and impair our abilities to use reading to engage the promise of democracy— that all "individuals should have the possibility to organize their lives as they wish, to choose their own ends, and to realize them as they think best" (Mouffe, 1996, p. 20). Acquiring and demonstrating these forms of common sense might be useful later to gain employment, membership, or status, but they are not social practices that will disrupt the common sense of exclusion expressed and implied in Locke's statement or help us to imagine how more diverse groups—the poor and others yet to be formed—can participate actively and equally in America becoming more democratic. For that, we need forms of reading that are wide awake to how representation, framing, and ideology work in society; to how plurality is the dynamic force of democracy; and to how every moment holds the opportunity for us to reconsider how we do things, why we do them, and what they accomplish and prevent (Shannon, 2011).

Those are the forms of reading—influenced by and influencing theories of radical democracy—I intend to demonstrate in this book and, then, tie to appropriate iterations of reading education. Scientific reading panels, common core standards, national testing, and a reading list of virtues separate us from decision making, telling us that we don't know enough to participate in the decisions that affect our lives and discouraging us from asking too many questions. They provide a reading education of social competence—of fitting into already established schemes of democracy. As those groups who won civil rights previously have demonstrated for us, as human beings, we all know enough and are capable of participating actively and effectively in civic life. Reading education should affirm those facts daily, developing social practices of exploring and acting on the complex relationships between the personal and the social. Reading wide awake does not guarantee this outcome, but it enables us to participate in Americans becoming more democratic in more parts of our lives.

> We can do better. We have done better before and other leading industrialized democracies are doing better now. Let's get started while the vast disparities in how people live and what they have still have the power to offend our sense of fair play. The worst thing we could do is get used to it. (Noah, 2012, p. 195)

2
CONDITIONS AND CONSEQUENCES

According to the *New York Times*, "no one seriously disputes the fact that students from disadvantaged households perform less well in school" (Ladd & Fiske, 2011, A23). Consider Ladd and Fiske's choice of words. They use "disadvantaged households" to represent the poor. Disadvantage denotes a competition in which groups are placed systematically into a hierarchy for a likely outcome. If one group is disadvantaged, then another must have an advantage. Ladd and Fiske name schooling as the field of competition. The students from higher-income families have an advantage over the poor and low-income students in school outcomes, they argue—and no one seriously disputes this fact. Think about that. If everyone knows about the disadvantage and advantage in schooling, but opportunities in public education are supposed to be fair, then someone or some group should be developing compensations to level the playing field among competitors. Accommodations should be made for those who are acknowledged to be disadvantaged and/or barriers should be placed before the advantaged to limit their edge. To do otherwise would be to make a mockery of equal opportunity in American education.

By choosing disadvantage to represent the poor and low-income students, Ladd and Fiske frame poverty as the result of systematic inequality in education that everyone acknowledges. Their choice of words guides our understanding of the issue and tells us about the ideology behind their choices. In this chapter I first work to put depth behind our understandings of what Ladd and Fiske say "everyone" seems to agree on—how poverty is defined; who are considered poor; and when, where, and how they are poor. Second, I examine how the federal government addresses poverty through direct and indirect aid. Third, I consider relationships between low income and performance in schools. I wonder why Ladd, Fiske, and others chose that order in the relationship—implying that individuals fail the institution—rather than reversing it to convey that the institution performs poorly toward disadvantaged households and their children. I find these issues to be both complex and contentious.

Ladd and Fiske's op-ed article is titled "Class Matters: Why Won't We Admit It?" I'm not certain if they chose the title for themselves or if a *Times* editor supplied it for them. The association of "class" with "disadvantage" expands the fields of competition to include income and wealth as well as education. Those losing the income competition perform less well in school. Why we won't admit that class matters, while no one seriously disputes the fact, could have something to do with the Marxian connotation of that term. In the 19th century, Marx wrote that class was determined through one's relationship to the means to produce commodities in order to sustain his or her life. Owners of the means of production formed one class with common interests to maintain the protection of property (acquired from profits). Everyone else in society comprised another class with common interests in recovering those profits that they created (through surplus value) when, in order to sustain themselves, they became commodities and sold their labor to owners. The tensions between classes are obvious, and Marx argued that if producers of profits (not the appropriators of them) became conscious of their class's creative capacities and collective power, then income and wealth would be distributed fairly among all. Class, when linked to inequality, then, evokes thoughts of revolution for many. It could be why owners and politicians cry, "class warfare" when anyone speaks or writes about inequality in America.

The words *poverty*, *class*, and *inequality* are tamed in the ways that the U.S. government officially describes the distribution of income in the United States. Rather than tie the distribution to any explicit theory, the government divides the population into fifths (quintiles) and reports on the income range and means for each 20 percent. The statistics and the neat boundaries make the distribution seem objective and natural. Although the official labels for these fifths vary across government documents, the intent is to pull perceptions toward the center—bottom, lower, middle, upper, and top. In 2011 (data released in September 2012) each quintile was comprised of approximately 24 million households with the following distribution of incomes.

2012 Household Income

Fifth	Range	Mean
Bottom	0–$20,259	$11,204
Lower	$20,260–$38,524	$29,204
Middle	$38,515–$62,433	$49,842
Upper	$62,434–$101,576	$80,080
Top	$101,577 and higher	$178,020

While the ranges appear relatively equal, the means show a different picture. For example, households at the top have a lower range only five times greater than the highest range for the households at the bottom ($101,577 to $20,259). A five-to-one ratio doesn't sound like inequality. The top mean, however, is almost 17 times larger than the bottom mean. That ratio suggests greater income disparity between the top and bottom. (When I wrote the first edition of this book, that ratio was 13.5 to 1.) The distribution of the U.S. aggregate income across each quintile tells the same story as the means in different way. In 2011 the bottom households shared 3.2 percent of the total amount of income in America and the top shared 51.1 percent of that total. The U.S. Census Bureau reports that the top 5 percent of households lived on more income than the bottom 50 percent of households.

These different ways of representing the distribution of income have led others to provide different divisions and labels to American classes. In *American Class Structure in an Age of Growing Inequality,* Dennis Gilbert (2002) named the classes: Capitalist (1 percent), Upper Middle (15 percent), Middle (60 percent), Working (13 percent), and Poor (12 percent). He argued that the working-class incomes are sufficiently fragile to make the line porous between working-class and poor households. Circumstances determined if the working class or poor would be above or below that line during any given month. Thompson and Hickey (2004) applied almost identical labels as Gilbert, but argued that over 30 percent of American households are working class and 20 percent live in poverty. For them, 50 percent of American households struggle to sustain themselves all or some times during a year. Beeghley (2004) provided a greater range for his middle group, calling the significant categories—the Super Rich (1 percent), Rich (5 percent), Middle (40 percent), Working (32 percent), and Poor (12 percent). Using 2007 data on wealth in America (income plus pensions, stocks and bonds, and homes), Kevin Drum (2011) returned to Marxist-like categories in which the top 10 percent of American households (the Rich) control over two-thirds of all the wealth in America, leaving one-third for the remaining 90 percent (the Rest).

Others have reached into the lower two categories to represent the income parameters of being poor. At the National Poverty Center at the University of Michigan, Shaefer and Edin (2012) developed the category of "extreme poverty," reporting that 2.8 million American children (are members of 1.46 million families who) live on less than $2 a day. To provide some perspective on that income, $2 a day is the amount the World Bank uses to describe "global poverty." The World Bank (2013) stated that such poverty is waning around the world, but Shaefer and Edin identified a 130 percent increase in American "global poverty" since 1996 (when the federal government ended "welfare as we know it"). Others assign the extreme term to any individual or family that lives on an income of less than half of the amount set as the official poverty line (Berube, Kneebone, & Nadeau, 2011). The *New York Times* coined the term "near poor" to represent households with incomes less than 150 percent of the official poverty line (Deparle, Gebeloff, & Tavernise, 2011). The group included 51 million Americans (less than $83 a day for a family of four for all expenses). According to the U.S. Census Bureau (2012), 39 percent of all children live in extreme, official, or near poverty.

Where class lines are drawn to establish categories of income and wealth, and which labels are affixed, influences our perceptions of poverty. As Kristof, Ladd, Fiske, government officials, and their revisionists demonstrate, the lines and labels are social constructions and are not descriptions of nature and evolution. Ideological decisions on where to draw and what to name classes offer Americans social positions meant to teach us who we are, what relationships we have with one another, and how we might act. For example, contrast Governor Romney's 47 percent "Takers" class who are dependent on government and feel entitled with Drum's 10 percent "Rich" class who control two-thirds of the wealth in America and who believe they are personally responsible for their success. Romney teaches us to see ourselves as among the 53 percent producers, to deplore the "moochers," and to end the government programs that favor (and ruin) those others. Drum instructs us to side with the 90 percent, to identify the imbalance as unjust, and to return to progressive practices in order to redistribute wealth.

In *The Submerged State,* Susan Mettler (2011) explains how the relative power of these ideologies influences Americans' perceptions of class, relationships, and actions. Since the 1980s, standard social benefits—Social Security, Medicare, welfare—have leveled off or declined, while tax expenditures—home mortgage interest deductions, low tax rates for capital gains, and tax deductions for charitable contributions—have increased substantially in number and amount. She documents an 86 percent increase in number and a growth in size to 7.4 percent of gross domestic product (GDP) (by contrast Social Security is 4.3 percent of the GDP). Mettler argues that because social benefits are direct payments, the public recognizes them as government support for the poor, while the largely invisible tax expenditures that benefit more affluent Americans are rarely questioned. As a result, many Americans misunderstand which classes receive benefits from the government, their relationships to these benefits, and how government actions contribute systematically to advantage and disadvantage within the income/ wealth and education competitions. For example, in a 2008 survey Mettler found 60 percent of those who received home mortgage interest deductions denied that they had ever used a government social program or that government had ever contributed to their economic well-being in any way. In a separate survey in which she provided more information about direct and submerged programs and identified who benefited from each, she discovered that Americans of all classes were more likely to favor government actions designed to decrease disadvantage and to object to those that increased advantage. Direct clear discussion of class, relationships, and actions, then, led to better understandings and more interest in democratic action.

How Is Poverty Defined?

Poverty is generally understood as insufficient income to sustain one's well-being. Perhaps you can identify the places where ideologies might clash over that statement. What do insufficient, sustain, and well-being mean? And when government officials first worked to establish the official poverty line in 1963, they engaged in just such disagreements.

> [The Saturday Group of the Council of Economic Advisors] would get into discussions about the definition of poverty. What kind of a concept and what kind of a number frame would you have in mind? Some people would say poverty obviously means lack of money income. That had the great merit of being something we had some numbers on. We could say how many people there were above and below some line and where they were and so on. But other people said that's really not what poverty means; poverty is more or sometimes less than money. It's a spiritual concept; or it's a participation-in-government concept; or it's a lack of some kind of self-esteem, sort of a psychological or image problem that people had. Or people would say, well, it really has to do with race; it has to do with sort of a near caste system in the United States. Still others would say it really has to do with lack of opportunity. It has to do with lack of facilities like schools and so on. That's what makes people really poor. . . . So there was a kind of sociological theory of poverty with its lack of remedies, and the economic theory with easy optimism that you could do something about it all. (Robert Lampman, Council of Economic Advisors from 1962 to 1964, as quoted in Gillette, 1996, pp. 6–7)

At that time, the Council of Economic Advisors chose an economic path to follow based on Mollie Orshansky's report to the U.S. Department of Agriculture (USDA). Through surveys, Orshansky concluded that the average family spent one-third of its income to feed itself and two-thirds on the remaining essentials (housing, utilities, health care, transportation, insurance, clothing, child care, education, the list goes on). The formula to establish poverty thresholds, then, would be simple—the cost of food per day × 365 × 3. Orshansky determined that a typical family of four could prepare minimally adequate meals each day for exactly $2.736, leading the Council to establish the poverty threshold for a family of four at $3,000 (2.736 × 365 = $998.84 × 3 = $2,995.92). The thresholds for families of different sizes were extrapolated from that figure, and those thresholds have retained that formula and ratio ever since (adjusted only for the rate of inflation each year and recently to include age of recipient as well). We can get a sense of the official thresholds (U.S. Census Bureau, 2012) from the following chart.

14 Conditions and Consequences

Size of Family	Weighted Average	With Children under 18
1	11,484	
1 (under 65)	11,702	
1 (65 or over)	10,788	
2	14,657	
2 (under 65)	15,139	15,504
2 (65 or over)	13,596	15,446
3	17,916	18,123 (one adult)
4	23,021	22,811 (two adults)
5	27,251	26,434 (one adult)
6	30,847	30,056 (two adults)
7	35,085	32,340 (one adult)
8	39,064	37,011 (two adults)
9 (or more)	46,572	43,487 (one adult)

The Census Bureau uses these thresholds to calculate official poverty statistics. It's called an *absolute measure* because it serves as a sharp cutoff, establishing clearly who are above or who are below these lines. The Department of Health and Human Services (HHS) determines poverty guidelines from these thresholds in order to establish an individual's financial eligibility for federal assistance programs. The guidelines consider family size and geography (Alaska and Hawaii have different scales than the 48 contiguous states and Washington, D.C.). They are not adjusted, however, according to the age of recipients. The differences between thresholds and guidelines seem slight. In 2012 the guidelines were $11,170 for a single individual, $23,050 for a family of four, and $34,930 for a household of seven. Guidelines are higher for Hawaiians and Alaskans, respectively, due to the cost of living in those states. The federal government's notes on thresholds and guidelines offer little explanation for the apparent duplication of efforts beyond the fact that different federal departments control these responsibilities of government.

Advocates of different ideologies object to the current thresholds and guidelines. For example, in *The Basic Economic Security Tables for the United States* (Kuriansky, 2013), the liberal organization Wider Opportunities for Women (WOW) argued that the basic poverty formula based on one-third for food for calculating thresholds is now deeply flawed because food costs have decreased as a percentage of family budgets (now estimated to be one-seventh of a family budget [Fass, 2009]), while other expenses have increased sharply. According to the organization's surveys, the costs of food, housing, and health care alone consume the entire budget as assumed under official poverty thresholds, leaving utilities, transportation, child care, and education uncovered. WOW advocates that the thresholds be raised dramatically in order to enable American families to sustain themselves and have a possibility of social mobility. Instead of $22,050 (in 2010 figures) as the absolute measure of poverty threshold for a family of four, WOW argued that the cutoff be set at $71,664. Otherwise, they explained, the family will be in jeopardy of not being able "to make ends meet" several months during the year.

Robert Rector and Rachel Sheffield (2011), from the conservative Heritage Foundation, reported that only a few Americans have "an inability to provide nutritious food, clothing, and reasonable shelter for one's family" (p. 1). Rather, for decades, they stated, the living conditions of the poor have steadily improved through access to higher wages and federal and state assistance programs to a point at which now many poor families can afford what were once considered to be luxury items—80 percent of poor households have air conditioning (in 1970, 36 percent of all American households enjoyed that service), nearly 75 percent own a car or truck, more than 50 percent have video game systems, and 43 percent have Internet access. Based on this information, Rector and Sheffield advocated that federal officials set thresholds and guidelines after considering all sources of income, including the income equivalent of assistance programs (tax credits, food support, and housing credits).

In 1990 the U.S. Congress commissioned "an independent scientific study of the concepts, measurement methods, and information needed for a poverty measure" (Short, 2012, p. 1), and in 1995 the National Academy of Sciences published that study, "Measuring Poverty: A New Approach" (Citro & Michael, 1995). In 2011 the U.S. Census Bureau produced a new statistic, the Supplemental Poverty Measure (SPM). Without attribution to the ideological critiques, the new measure counts direct federal assistance payments and tax credits as income, (conservative suggestions), but it subtracts from income certain out-of-pocket medical costs, other work-related expenses (child care, education), and taxes paid (liberal suggestions). Moreover, the new supplemental measures are adjusted for cost-of-living differences by region (liberal and conservative suggestion). The SPM is not intended to supplant the official thresholds, and it cannot be used as guidelines for eligibility for federal assistance programs. It simply provides more information (Short, 2012). For comparison, in 2011 the official threshold for a family of four was $22,811 (two adults and two children) and the supplemental measures were $25,703 (house owners with a mortgage), $21,175 (owners without a mortgage), and $25,222 (renters).

Who Are Considered Poor?

Using the SPM the Census Bureau divides Americans into four categories relative to the official poverty line (Tritch, 2011). This choice gives a different feel to the distribution of income in America than the official quintiles. First, the change suggests relationships among all Americans—the poverty line connects us. Second, although at first glance there appears to be progress toward income equality, the choice of ranges actually doesn't reveal that information. Yes, the ratio of the lower limit of being well off is only four times higher than the upper limit of being poor—it is five to one for the quintiles—however, the SPM does not specify the mean income for each class. We can't determine if the quintiles' ratio of 17 to 1 for means holds for SPM. Third, although the middle class is nearly 15 percent larger in the new distribution than it is in the quintile form, the middle is no longer at the center of the income distribution. Of American households, 47.9 percent are assigned to poor and low categories, and only 17.3 percent are considered to be well off and above the middle class. SPM distribution, then, gives the impression that nearly half of Americans struggle to make ends meet.

SPM Income Distribution (2011)

Poor (below the poverty line)	16.1 percent of the population
Low (from one to two times above)	31.8 percent
Middle (from two to four times above)	34.8 percent
Well off (over four times above)	17.3 percent

Despite the variation, all official statistical accounts represent the poor as if poverty defined them completely and as if they were a monolithic group. Individuals living below the poverty line are as diverse as those in any other class, although poverty is not spread evenly, or even proportionately, among groups of Americans. Women, minorities, the young, southerners, and urban dwellers are more likely to be poor and to stay poor longer.

Adult women are more likely to be poor than men—the poverty rates are 14.6 percent for women and 10.9 percent for men (U.S. Census Bureau, 2011b). This gender disadvantage has been consistent since the official statistics began in 1965. Although the gender pay gap has closed over the last 50 years, women are still paid only 77 percent of what men are paid and, therefore, employed females are 38 percent more likely to be poor than males. The gender poverty gap holds true across all levels of education, from a 40 percent gap between adults who did not finish high school to a 13 percent divide for those who graduated from college. In 2011, 31.2 percent of families with female householders and 16.1 percent of families with male householders lived in poverty (U.S. Census Bureau, 2012). Women lead 85 percent of single-parent households in the United States (Glynn, 2012). Children living in single-female-headed families are eight times more likely to live in extreme poverty than children living with married couples (National Center for Law and Economic Justice, 2013).

According to the U.S. Census Bureau (2012, Table 711), the majority of poor Americans are White. There are three times as many poor White Americans as poor African Americans and twice as many as poor Hispanic Americans. Yet, African Americans and Hispanic Americans are overrepresented among the poor. Although African Americans represent only 13 percent of the general population and Hispanic Americans comprise only 17 percent, more than one in four African Americans and nearly one in four Hispanic Americans are poor (National Center for Law and Economic Justice, 2013). Again, a gap in wages contributes to the greater likelihood of being poor. The median weekly wages for African American and Hispanic American workers are 65 percent and 61 percent of White workers' wages, respectively (U.S. Census Bureau, 2012, Table 701). Beyond income, there is a gap in wealth as well—White Americans have 22 times the wealth of African Americans and 15 times that of Hispanic Americans (Luhby, 2012). And despite claims of Americans being self-made economically, there is a racial/ethnic gap for inheritance as well—1 in 3 White Americans will inherit substantial wealth during their lifetimes, while only 1 in 10 African Americans or Hispanic Americans is likely to receive a financial inheritance.

Poverty rates for all age groups have declined since 1959 when 37 percent of the elderly, 27 percent of children, and 18 percent of adults were recognized as poor. According to a Congressional Report (Gabe, 2012), the elderly have experienced the most dramatic drop, to 8.7 percent in 2011. Rates for children and adults decreased to 22 and 14 percent, respectively. Children are now the poorest age group in America, followed by youth between ages 18 and 25, who are experiencing unemployment rates over 25 percent nationally and over 50 percent in some urban and rural areas. The age of children and youth is a factor in poverty as well. Twenty-six percent of all children under age 3 years are poor; 25 percent of children ages 3–5; 22 percent of children ages 6–11, and 19 percent of all children ages 12–17 live in poor families. One in 10 children live in extreme poverty, with only 61 percent of that group receiving government cash assistance from Temporary Assistance for Needy Families (TANF) (Children's Defense Fund, 2013).

In 2011 poverty was spread relatively evenly across regions of the United States (south 16.1 percent, west 15.9 percent, midwest 14 percent, and northeast 13 percent). Roughly 47 percent of the poor live in large and small metropolitan areas, and 19.5 percent reside in rural areas (Luhby, 2012). Kneebone and Garr (2010) report on the accelerating rate of poverty in American suburbs. A record 15.4 million suburban residents—one-third of the nation's poor—lived below the poverty line in 2010, up 11 percent from the year before. The Brookings Institute (Berube et al., 2011) noted a 33 percent rise in poor families who live in concentrated poverty (areas where more that 40 percent of residents are poor), explaining that concentrated poverty means a lower tax base to support civic institutions (schools, hospitals, public transportation, police, and fire stations), lower retail service (grocery stores, banks, and pharmacies), and fewer employment opportunities. Although urban areas still suffer the greatest concentration, suburban areas of concentrated poverty are increasing more rapidly in the wake of the Great Recession.

For many in the United States, poverty is a temporary condition. Families experience spells of poverty followed by periods of low income across their lifetime. According to the *Dynamics of Economic Well-Being 2004–2006* report (U.S. Census

Bureau, 2011a), 23 percent of families remained in poverty during the entire 36-month period studied. Although 77 percent exited poverty during the three years, their upward mobility was often not permanent. For example, 42 percent of the original group reported being out of poverty in 2006 when the survey ended. The remaining 35 percent, who exited poverty at least once during the three years, had dropped back below the poverty line by 2006. According to these data, the SPM's blurring of the line between the poor and low classes seems not only justified, but a more accurate representation of poverty in America than either the quintiles or the official thresholds.

In the *Dynamics* study, the Census Bureau found that the median length of a spell of poverty was 4.5 months. Children (5.2 months) and the elderly (6.7 months) remained poor longer than working-aged adults. Among the households that exited poverty during the three years, over 50 percent experienced repeated spells of poverty because their household incomes never exceeded near poverty (150 percent of official poverty threshold), and their lack of wealth made them ill prepared for unforeseen circumstances—household events (e.g., illness or accident), economic events (e.g., businesses moving or contracting in recession or prices rising during economic boom), or natural events (e.g., drought or catastrophic weather).

This fact of fluctuation between being poor and low income contradicts the ideas of America as a land of opportunity and upward mobility. During the 40 years following the Great Depression, it was true that children would eventually exceed the income of their parents, if not move between official classes. Yet, the Economic Mobility Project at the Brookings Institute (Issacs, Sawhill, & Haskins, 2008) has concluded that the United States is the most class-bound society among Western nations. (And conservatives believe this to be true as well [Winship, 2011].) Although some children living in poverty or within low-income families might move to the middle class (26 percent) or even above (4 percent), they are much more likely to remain in the same economic class as their parents (70 percent) (Currier, 2012).

These demographic categories (gender, race/ethnicity, age, region, and residence) combine in unique ways for poor individuals, disrupting the notion that anyone can be defined by poverty alone and making assistance programs complex indeed. This fact challenges the stereotypes of the "generational poor" that animate the antipoverty programs in many schools (Payne, 2005). Across all regions, White children comprise the largest number of poor children, but a startling 65 percent of African American and Hispanic American children live in low-income and poor families; 39 percent of poor children live in families making payments toward home ownership, but 62 percent of low-income children moved within the last year; 37 percent of poor children have married parents living in the household; and 72 percent live in homes with at least one adult employed 40 hours a week (Addy, Engelhart, & Skinner, 2013; Chau, Thampi, & Wight, 2010). Within the dynamic nature of American poverty,

72 million American children have a chance of experiencing the conditions of poverty during any given month.

What Are Federal Assistance Programs?

Because the U.S. Constitution does not address the topic of poverty directly, federal officials use a combination of two Constitutional clauses to take some responsibility for citizens' well-being. The General Welfare Clause enables the federal government to tax and spend in order to accomplish its goals, and the Commerce Clause enables Congress to regulate interstate economic activity. The combination is the legal justification for federal public accommodation laws, including protections for the environment, civil rights, health, and education. Such laws address problems that require coordination among states to reach national solutions. Of course, debate about the use of these legislative powers is as old as the Constitution, trying to find balances between federal jurisdiction and state rights and individualism and common good.

Since the Great Depression, the federal government has used these clauses to weave a social safety net that is intended to keep individuals from falling too deeply into economic distress, causing immediate or future restraint on the economic productivity of the nation. The size of that net, its weavers, and its consequences for individuals and the country remain points of contention even 80 years later. Arguments arise over who should be eligible, what should be covered, and who should regulate the net. Currently, five federal departments and two service agencies use the HHS Poverty Guidelines, or means-testing, to determine families' eligibility for assistance programs in eight broad categories: health care, income, food, housing, education, social services, energy, and employment and training.

Eligibility is determined by either a simple comparison of family income to the HHS Poverty Guidelines (or more recently a multiple ranging from 125 percent to 200 percent) or a means-tested comparison in which a family must demonstrate a need for the particular service and the inability to pay for it. For some programs, if found to be eligible, a family becomes legally entitled to the benefit. Entitlement safety-net programs—Social Security, Medicare, Medicaid, Supplemental Nutritional Assistance Program (SNAP; food stamps), TANF (welfare), and unemployment benefits—can create difficulties for establishing federal and state budgets because the number of needy and eligible families is difficult to predict and is subject to fluctuations in the economy. For example, eligibility for SNAP rose sharply during the Great Recession, exceeding its anticipated budget lines. Other discretionary poverty programs in the safety net—education programs, job training, and housing—are funded annually at a specific amount of the federal budget. Often, not all eligible families receive benefits from discretionary programs because funds become depleted before all eligible households can be served.

A few parts of the safety net are direct transactions between the federal government and individuals. Social Security is the prime example—most workers are required to pay Social Security taxes as a retirement plan, and then become entitled to those funds (plus interest) when they choose to retire. If a participant dies before retirement, the spouse and children are eligible for Social Security payments to compensate for loss of the deceased's income. Most assistance programs are partnerships between federal and state authorities in which states must meet general federal parameters in order to qualify for federal funding, but state officials can interpret those parameters in order to fit the circumstances within their boundaries. HHS's Head Start is a shared-responsibility assistance program, and individual Head Start schools demonstrate state and local interpretation while meeting federal guidelines and augmenting federal funds. In some states, private agencies and businesses perform these services under both state and federal supervision. These private charities serve important functions in confronting poverty, but their decisions and services need only meet federal guidelines if they accept federal funding. Federal regulations to engender equal treatment sometimes cause considerable controversy. Think, for example, of Catholic hospitals' and agencies' concerns over federal requirements to supply birth control for workers and clients, or even the federal government's reluctance to offer benefit rights to the gay and lesbian spouses and partners of employees.

The federal safety net has considerable reach. According to a Pew Research Center study, 71 percent of Americans live in households that at least one time received assistance through the federal safety net (Morin, Taylor, & Patten, 2012). Fifty-five percent acknowledged personal benefit from one or more of the six entitlement programs, and the rest reported that a member of their nuclear family so benefited. (Twenty-seven percent have collected unemployment assistance, 26 percent Social Security payment, 22 percent Medicare, 18 percent SNAP, 11 percent Medicaid, and 8 percent TANF.) Acknowledgements of benefits cut across political lines—57 percent of conservatives and 53 percent of both liberals and moderates claimed benefits. Applications for assistance begin early in adult life with a third of all young adults (ages 18–29) claiming receipt, and they rise steadily (45 percent for 30- and 40-somethings and 54 percent of Americans between ages 50 and 64) until age 65 and after, when they reach 97 percent through Social Security and/or Medicare. Rural residents benefit disproportionately from entitlements (62 percent) when compared to urban (54 percent) and suburban dwellers (53 percent). Regardless of whether an individual (or household) has received benefits, nearly 6 in 10 agreed that the federal and state governments should provide a safety net of services for the needy.

This placement of a safety net under so many Americans is controversial, however. While virtually everyone believes that temporary assistance to families in need is an important societal responsibility, some worry about the length of assistance, the expense, and the displacement of support for the truly disadvantaged. Bentele (2012) points with some satisfaction to the successful elasticity of the safety net during the first two years of the Great Recession (2007–2009), demonstrating that SNAP, unemployment insurance, TANF, and tax cuts combined to keep many lower and some middle-class Americans from falling below the poverty line. But he shows how the variability among states was so great that the poor experienced the largest and the smallest declines in income among classes, depending on their state of residence. Armor and Sousa (2012) examined the same numbers as Bentele and deplored the spread of benefits to households with incomes more than 200 percent of the HHS Poverty Guidelines. They argued that those families should have been forced to use their wealth when income dropped, concluding that they "took advantage" of the system. In testimony before the House of Representatives, Ron Haskins (2012), co-director of the Brookings Institution's Center for Children and Families, commented on the need for clear phase-out procedures for federal assistance benefits in order to provide an incentive to work. In a similar manner, Aaron (2013) called for stiffer eligibility rules in order to control both demand for and cost of assistance. And Sherman, Greenstein, and Ruffing (2012) emphasized that nine-tenths of these entitlement benefits were awarded to the elderly, disabled, or working families, displacing needed support for children living in poor and low-income households.

The Safety Net for Children

The Great Recession (officially from 2007 to 2009) tested the strengths and exposed some of the weaknesses of the social safety net for children. Wheaton, Giannarellie, Martinez-Schiferl, and Zedlewski (2011) found that tax credits, SNAP, and housing subsidies had strong preventative effects. Without the Earned Income Tax Credit (EITC) program, for example, the child poverty rate would have been four percentage points higher and three points higher still without SNAP (that would be a 29 percent child poverty rate). Families receiving Medicaid assistance were more likely to report that their children were receiving preventative medical care, that their children's health was good, and that their family was more financially secure than low-income families without Medicaid benefits (Finkelstein et al., 2011). Extended unemployment insurance benefits through the American Recovery and Reinvestment Act of 2009 kept 3.4 million families out of poverty (Sherman, 2011). However, the Great Recession had a severely negative impact on state budgets, causing large cuts in funding for social services within the safety nets in many states (Skinner, 2012). The result was greater variation of support for poor and low-income children across states.

Medicaid is a shared low-cost public-health entitlement program designed to support the health care of poor and low-income families with children. The federal government sets minimum standards for eligibility, which states can expand. Federal funding is weighted toward states with greater need and was increased substantially under the Federal Recovery and Reinvestment Act of 2009 and the Affordable Care Act of 2010. In 2010 nearly one-fourth of all Americans lived in households in which at least one member received Medicaid benefits (U.S. Census Bureau, 2011b).

For children whose family's income exceeds Medicaid eligibility, states offer shared Child Health Insurance Programs (CHIP). These are discretionary programs (not entitlements) that are subject to annual funding caps—that is, CHIP can and do leave some eligible children uncovered each year. CHIP are funded through a three-to-one ratio of federal to state dollars. On average, 85 percent of eligible children receive CHIP benefits, but some states report remarkably lower participation rates (Centers for Medicare and Medicaid Services, 2011). This leads to acrimony between state and federal officials (Goodnough, 2013). The Affordable Care Act requires nearly all Americans to have private health insurance, offering tax credits for those who can't afford to join employer-sponsored, group insurance programs. However, eligibility for those credits is based only on the cost of individual coverage, and not on the more expensive family plans. Executive Director of the Center for Children and Families, Jocelyn Guyer, stated: "This is bad news for kids" (as quoted in Pear, 2013).

SNAP is a shared entitlement program that provides poor and low-income households with a monthly dollar allotment on a special debit card that can be used to purchase food. The federal government fully funds the benefit costs and half the administrative costs of this program. States are obligated to fund the other half of the administration. States can extend SNAP benefits beyond the federal minimum and/or lower the eligibility guidelines. In 2011 more than 14 percent of all American households participated in SNAP programs—a 70 percent increase since 2007 with funding more than doubling. Ninety-two percent of eligible families with children participate. Yet, federal and state proposals to balance budgets frequently include proposals to reduce SNAP programs through more stringent eligibility requirements and cuts in benefits (Rosenbaum, 2012).

Originally started during the Great Depression in order support crop prices and feed hungry children at school, the *National School Lunch Program* (1946) provides free breakfasts, lunches, and afterschool snacks to children living in households with incomes below 130 percent of the poverty threshold and at reduced costs to children from households with incomes below 185 percent. This is now a shared entitlement program (the funding is 70 percent federal and 30 percent state). Of the 5 billion federal meals provided to 31 million students across the United States, 59 percent were free, 9 percent were reduced, and 33 percent were purchased (Federal Education Budget Project, 2013). Thirty percent of the school lunches meet federal nutritional guidelines, and critics call for more nutritious food in smaller portions. Educational researchers often use eligibility for free and reduced lunch as a marker for poverty (National Center for Education Statistics, 2012); however, because free and reduced lunch programs require families to complete applications, this marker is likely to underestimate the numbers of poor and low-income students.

The *Department of Housing and Urban Development* (HUD) offers over one million units of government-owned public housing across the United States. Thirty percent of the residents must have incomes below the poverty threshold, and there are income eligibility restrictions on the remaining 70 percent. Sixty percent of the public units are located outside of areas with concentrated poverty rates. Residents must abide by a code of conduct and contribute the larger of either 30 percent of their income or $50 ("minimum rent"). Children reside in 40 percent of these units. *Section 8 of the Low Income Housing Assistance* began during the Great Depression, providing vouchers for poor and low-income families to assist them in securing safe and affordable housing. The vouchers are a shared, discretionary program in which families must demonstrate both a need and a lack of income/wealth to pay for private-sector housing. Over two million families receive vouchers under roughly the same rules as residents in public housing. According to the Center for Budget and Policy Priorities (2013), 52 percent of vouchers are awarded to families with children. According to hud.gov (2013), however:

> Since the demand for housing assistance often exceeds the limited resources available to HUD and the local housing agencies, long waiting periods are common. In fact, a PHA may close its waiting list when it has more families on the list than can be assisted in the near future.
>
> PHAs may establish local preferences for selecting applicants from its waiting list. For example, PHAs may give a preference to a family who is (1) homeless or living in substandard housing, (2) paying more than 50% of its income for rent, or (3) involuntarily displaced. Families who qualify for any such local preferences move ahead of other families on the list who do not qualify for any preference. Each PHA has the discretion to establish local preferences to reflect the housing needs and priorities of its particular community.

The federal government provides tax credits to poor and low-income households. The *Child Tax Credit* provides up to $1,000 per child and can be redeemed as cash if the amount exceeds a household's tax liability. The value of the credit declines as the household income rises above a threshold. The American Recovery and Reinvestment Act expanded this credit by $15 billion in an attempt to keep low-income families' incomes steady. The *Child and Dependent Care Tax Credit* supports up to 35 percent of child care during working hours for households with earned incomes. This credit is not an entitlement and cannot be redeemed as cash for general childcare expenses. The safety net also includes direct payment support for child care to low-income working parents whose income does not exceed 85 percent of the state's median income. This benefit is not an entitlement, and only about 17 percent of the eligible families receive these subsidies. The *EITC* was enacted in 1975 and was expanded greatly in scope in 1996 when "welfare as we know it" ended. EITC is now the largest cash support program for low-income and poor families, returning more that $59 billion to more than 26 million families in 2011. Twenty-two states have their own versions of EITC. Federal and state governments combine to offer *unemployment insurance* (UI), a modest, time-limited, weekly cash stipend to qualified workers who lose their jobs through no fault of their own. Part-time, temporary, and self-employed workers are not qualified for the UI entitlement. During the Great Recession, the typical 26-week benefit period was extended several times until it reached 99 weeks in 2012.

"Welfare as we know it" became *Temporary Assistance for Needy Families* in 1996 in order to "increase the work incentive among the poor." TANF is a shared discretionary cash assistance program that is funded annually at $16.5 billion (since 1996) through federal block grants to states. State legislatures have significant control over benefit levels, work requirements, and time limits on benefit receipt. In some states TANF is connected to childcare subsidies, increasing substantially assistance to eligible families. In 1996, 61 percent of children living in poor households received welfare cash assistance; in 2008, 26.7 percent of poor children received TANF benefits. This is called the great success of welfare reform (Haskins, 2006). States vary greatly in the scope and generosity of benefits, ranging from 60 percent of children living in poverty receiving TANF cash in Rhode Island to only 3 percent receiving such benefits in Wyoming. Monthly allotments vary as well—with a single-parent family of three receiving $753 each month in New York City and $170 in Jackson, Mississippi.

In *So Rich So Poor,* Edelman (2012) argued that six million Americans live on SNAP benefits as their only income. Edelman resigned from the Clinton Administration when the Personal Responsibility and Work Opportunity Act (1996) replaced welfare with TANF. Before 1996, a cash poverty benefit had been an entitlement without preconditions; after the Act passed, individuals had to be employed or vigorously seeking employment in order to qualify for cash benefits without childcare benefits attached. Moreover, TANF became a federal block grant to states without a requirement that the funds must be allocated only as cash relief for the poor. This change provided state governments with an incentive to remove previously eligible families from the cash assistance in order to allocate the federal funds for other state needs. And this incentive seemed to have worked. Edelman (2012) reported that only 20 percent of eligible children receive TANF benefits in 19 states. During the Great Recession, when unemployment topped 10 percent, families were unable to qualify for TANF because less work was available, and they could not receive federal tax credits because they had little or no income on which to pay taxes. In these situations, their entitlement to SNAP benefits became their only access to income. Although these circumstances were atypical to be sure, they were spread across the United States (Deparle & Gebeloff, 2010). While before Congress, even Haskins (2012), who claimed that TANF has been successful before the Great Recession, admitted that the TANF program proved to be inadequate as the only cash benefit in the social safety net when work was/is not readily available.

As part of the Johnson Administration's War on Poverty, *Head Start* began as an experimental summer-school program to prepare poor four-year-olds for public school. Today, Head Start provides a wide range of services to low-income three- and four-year-olds and their families, including child cognitive and language development activities; medical, dental, and mental health services; and nutritional and social services. Federally funded, Head Start is not an entitlement and is subject to annual appropriations. Since Head Start began, the federal government has not provided sufficient funds to enroll all eligible children. In 2002 enrollment peaked at over 900,000 children. Waldfogel (2009) estimated that Head Start served half the eligible children. In 1994 *Early Head Start* was launched to provide services to eligible pregnant mothers until their child became eligible for Head Start. Less than 5 percent of the eligible mothers and children received benefits from this program (Schmitt, 2011). Forty states have pre-kindergarten programs for low-income children. Twenty-one operate means-tested programs, and 19 provide universal pre-kindergarten programs regardless of family income. Over one million children are enrolled in state programs (Barnett, 2010). In his 2013 State of the Union Address, President Obama called for universal preschool for poor and low-income four-year-old children—several steps shy of Senator Mondale's 1971 bill for making quality preschools available to every family. President Nixon vetoed that bill, calling it a "communal approach to child rearing" (as quoted in Edelman, 2012, p. 74).

The social safety net for children is a complex mix of programs that provides health care, food, shelter, income, and education for those deemed to be most in need. Many children are helped in some, and sometimes several, ways, but some—too many—fall through the webbing or miss the net altogether because of circumstances not of their making. Federal entitlement and discretionary programs do not reach all eligible children, and state programs vary in their commitments to patch or extend the federal net to reach them all. As a consequence, children in poor and low-income households are sick, hungry, and tired more often than their middle-income and well-off peers, leaving the former with the disadvantage that suppresses their school performance, as Ladd and Fiske identified. Even those children who find the supports that enable their families to bounce above poverty thresholds can at times suffer the effects of poverty conditions.

What Are the Consequences of Poverty on Children's School Performance?

The type of research I'll use in this section cannot address specific children or contexts. Rather, this research addresses poverty in terms of general tendencies and probabilities. People living in poverty are diverse individuals who negotiate their lives in a variety of ways, and the effects of biological and social characteristics associated with poverty might not pertain to individual children. This being acknowledged, many scholars (see Duncan & Murnane, 2011) conclude that true disadvantage reduces children's opportunities and capacities to make the most of whatever happens at school. Statistically, poor and low-income children are more likely to have low birth weight, to be ill fed, to lack health care, to live in inadequate shelter, to feel unsafe and insecure, and to lack the expected dispositions and experiences for schooling. All interfere with learning and arise from the economic conditions of their daily lives.

Low birth weight is set at 5.5 pounds and is associated with prolonged and serious illness (asthma); infections (nose and throat); and motor (eye–hand coordination), social (externalizing aggression and/or internalizing anxiety), and cognitive delays (autism and lower intelligence) (Center for Disease Control and Prevention, 2012). Eight percent of American babies are born with low birth weight (Kaiser Family State Health Facts, 2012). Lower-income parents are twice as likely to have babies with low birth weight and four times more likely than wealthier parents to have children with very low (3.3 pounds) or extremely low (2.2 pounds) birth weight (typically due to premature births). Lighter babies are more likely to suffer multiple complications, and those complications are more likely to last into adolescence and adulthood (Cheadle & Goosby, 2010).

Food insecurity is a regular and sustained risk of a food supply sufficient to maintain one's health, development, and concentration. Children living in food-insecure households number 16.7 million (Coleman-Jensen, Nord, Andrews, & Carlson, 2012). Hungry children are more likely to be ill, absent, lethargic, and inattentive. Chronic hunger among infants and toddlers is associated with slower cognitive development and lower powers of concentration that last into adulthood (Wight, Thampi, & Briggs, 2010).

Lack of access to health care is directly and positively correlated with income (U.S. Census Bureau, 2011b). Despite CHIP, 10 percent of children lack health insurance of any kind (Children's Defense Fund, 2013). Poor children are more likely to have lower rates of immunization and fewer preventive checkups for treatable illness, vision problems, or dental health. They have less access to treatments for chronic conditions (asthma, diabetes) or to mental health services (Kaiser Family State Health Facts, 2012). Consequently, they are more likely to be sick when attending school or to be absent, causing "their educational achievement to suffer" (Bernstein, Chollet, & Peterson, 2010).

Inadequate housing is associated with greater chance of chronic illness, colds, and infections; exposure to toxins (lead and radon), damaging immune systems and cognitive functioning; sleep deprivation; and transience (Anatani, Chau, Wight, & Addy, 2011). Housing costs consume more than the 30 percent of low incomes recommended by the U.S. Department of Housing and Urban Development (Bravve, Bolton, Couch, & Crowley, 2012) and, therefore, low-income housing is more likely to be older, drafty, and cramped; to need repair; and to be located in less-safe neighborhoods. Six million families live in substandard housing (hud.gov, 2013).

Toxic stress is the continued activation of the genetically coded response system that prepares the body to engage temporal environmental challenges (Wilkerson & Pickett, 2009). Stress activates the nervous system and specific hormones that raise heart rate, breathing rate, blood pressure, and metabolism, enabling an individual to take on the challenge with enhanced focus, strength, stamina, and alertness until the challenge ends. Continued activation of the stress system, however, is toxic to the human body and disposition, leaving the individual feeling overwhelmed, weakening his or her immune system, and causing long-term degradation of cognitive functioning. Children living in poverty are more likely to demonstrate the physiological symptoms of toxic stress daily, even when there is no apparent challenge in their environment (Evans & Schamberg, 2009). As poverty persists through childhood and adolescence, the symptoms become more acute, suppressing working memory (Farah et al., 2006; Noble, Norman, & Farrah, 2005), influencing the structure of the brain (Nelson & Sheridan, 2011), and limiting the genetic expression of individuals (Nisbett, 2009). These consequences disrupt logical thinking, behavioral control, language comprehension, and reading.

In *So Much Reform, So Little Change*, Payne (2008) argues that social factors as well as biological factors inhibit the potential impact of school reforms for children in poverty. Segregated low-income communities have fewer institutional resources, fewer employment opportunities, greater concentrations of people suffering the biological effects of poverty on their minds and bodies, and less social cohesion, which demoralize families and paralyze their civic actions. Toxic stress and lack of resources affect family life. Poor children are less likely to be supervised, to talk with adults, to engage in literacy events, and to participate in academically enriching events and contexts in and outside the home (Phillips, 2011). These parenting styles and uses of time limit poor children's readiness for typical school curricula and subsequent academic achievement (Lareau, 2003). As Heath (1983) and Taylor and Dorsey-Gaines (1988) demonstrated decades ago and Compton-Lilly, Rogers, and Lewis (2012) explained more recently, however, these effects reflect as much on schooling and research epistemologies as they do on the potential of families living in poverty.

Statistically, low-income families are more verbally and physically violent, less cohesive, and less stable (Sedlak et al., 2010). Poor children are more likely to be exposed to smoking, drinking, and drug abuse, and they are more likely to live among people who believe themselves to be socially powerless (and act according to those beliefs). Members of low-income communities are less likely to trust and rely on others or feel secure when in public (Sastry & Pebley, 2010). Even if these consequences are not present in their family life, poor children learn to negotiate these practices and these environments in a variety of ways in order to be recognized as members within families.

Poverty takes a toll on children's bodies and minds and shapes their behavior in ways that interfere with their learning at school. This is not an excuse (Sanchez, 2013) but, rather, a research-based conclusion that children living in poverty are more likely to be in need of medical treatment, to be hungry and tired, to be absent, to suffer from cognitive and physical delays in development, to possess a smaller vocabulary, to lack expected general and school experiences, to exhibit disruptive behavior/sullen disposition, and to suffer less working memory and lower gene expression due to prolonged toxic stress. These are the general attributes hidden behind Ladd and Fiske's term *disadvantaged households*.

At the same time, members of classes with disposable income are pressing their advantage. Kaushal, Magnuson, and Waldgogel (2011) demonstrate that as income rises, families invest in their children by providing opportunities for "educational-related items and activities such as music and art lessons, children's books and toys, sports equipment and classes, and tutoring" (p. 187). These income-related opportunities prepare preschool children for school expectations, providing immediate intellectual, linguistic, social, and emotional assets at the beginning of schooling, and then, supplement and extend the in-school activities in ways unavailable to poor and low-income children and youth. Lareau (2011) suggests that these investments are intended to familiarize children with various social institutions and to prepare them to negotiate with the adults present in order to enhance the likelihood of positive outcomes. Over time, Lareau maintains, the parents and their children begin to shape the institutions' rules and practices in order to turn the economic advantage into a social edge as well. She uses schooling as the prime example of this unofficial collusion.

Ladd and Fiske argue that these advantages and disadvantages exist and that "no one seriously disputes the fact." According to liberal democratic theory, then, as the neutral arbiter, government should intervene in order to at least mute inequalities. Even Adam Smith in *The Wealth of Nations* (1776) invited government to temper "free markets" with moral regulations of fairness and justice. And in poorly coordinated, often uneven, and sometimes effective ways, U.S. governments have acted to temper the consequences of the economy for Americans through regulating business and commerce, taxing in order to devise a social safety net, and designing educational programs to end poverty. Yet as the Collaboration for Poverty Research (CRP) attests, governments do not appear to have the political will to be that neutral arbiter that uses moral regulations of fairness and justice to temper inequalities.

> Among those who regard poverty as a major social problem, the conventional view is that we should respond by declaring a new "war on poverty," then introduce initiatives that would lower the poverty rate, and thereby reduce the poverty rate in the U.S. However sensible such an approach may seem, there are real political hurdles that in the U.S. context make it difficult to take on poverty in any concerted way, and one might therefore focus additionally on measures that reduce the negative effects of poverty among those experiencing it. (Collaboration for Poverty Research, 2010)

The CPR is a joint effort of Stanford University and Harvard University faculties to address poverty from a scientific point of view with a focus on breaking the strong link between poverty and toxic stress and providing poor and low-income children with preschool language and cognitive experiences. This quote, however, suggests that they acknowledge that science does not necessarily determine government education policies (Shannon, 2007). CPR researchers seek to read the difference between the 1960s and now imaginatively ("declaring a new war on poverty"), but feel blocked by real political hurdles. Rather than "tak(ing) on poverty in any concerted way" by reading those political hurdles carefully and acting on them, they recommend steps to meliorate poverty's effects. While such acts are certainly welcomed, John Marsh labels such steps dangerous because they leave the power relations circulating in the same ways that have produced poverty in the past and maintain it in the present and apparently the future. Marsh quotes James Agee from *Let Us Now Praise Famous Men: Three Tenant Families*:

> It is dangerous because by wrong assignment of causes it persuades that the "cure" is possible through means which in fact would have little effect save to delude the saviors into the comfortable idea that nothing more needed doing, or even looking into. (Marsh, 2011, p. 212)

3
OPPORTUNITY
Liberals

To me, a liberal is one who believes in using, in a non-violent, tolerant and democratic way, the forces of education, publicity, politics, economics, business, law and religion to direct the ever-changing and increasing power of science into channels which will bring peace and the maximum of well-being both spiritual and economic to the greatest number of human beings. A liberal knows that the only certainty in this life is change, but believes that the change can be directed toward a constructive end. (Wallace, 1953)

If by a "Liberal" they mean someone who looks ahead and not behind, someone who welcomes new ideas without rigid reactions, someone who cares about the welfare of the people—their health, their housing, their schools, their jobs, their civil rights, and their civil liberties—someone who believes we can break through the stalemate and suspicions that grip us in our policies abroad, if that is what they mean by a "Liberal," then I'm proud to say I'm a "Liberal." (Kennedy, 1960)

The success of science depends on an apparatus of democratic adjudication—anonymous peer review, open debate, the fact that a graduate student can criticize a tenured professor. These mechanisms are more or less explicitly designed to counter human self-deception. People always think they're right, and powerful people will tend to use their authority to bolster their prestige and suppress inconvenient opposition. You try to set up the game of science so that the truth will out despite this ugly side of human nature. (Steven Pinker as quoted in Mooney, 2005)

I start with liberalism because much of the debate and action surrounding the relationship between poverty and reading education during the last three or four decades has been a reaction to liberals' attempts to represent and frame these issues during the 20th century. Liberals represent poverty as insufficient income to adequately care for oneself and one's family. They frame poverty as a lack of opportunity to participate effectively in societal structures and institutions designed to bring about economic success. Ideologically, liberals locate the causes of poverty predominantly outside the personal capabilities and responsibilities of individuals. Rather, liberals argue that people who are poor have been historically and systematically denied access to opportunity to prosper, and therefore, they benefit less and suffer more from the realities of a market economy.

According to liberal democratic theory, governments are the final arbiters of whether any route to specific opportunities is considered to be fair to all. When access is deemed unfair, government regulation should follow and temporary assistance programs should be offered to those who suffer most. All these principles are explicit in the quotes at the start of the chapter. Henry A. Wallace was one of Franklin Roosevelt's vice presidents and is credited with helping to design and implement the New Deal. Kennedy was the inspiration for both the Great Society and War on Poverty legislation in the 1960s. Pinker is a linguist and public intellectual within the current discussions of evidence and authority in issues of evolution and climate change. Like any group, liberals are diverse individuals, who share these representational, frame, and ideological commitments to varying degrees, and of course, liberals have enjoyed only limited social and political power across time. Conservatives and radicals contested liberal policies and practices throughout the 20th century.

The Collaboration for Poverty Research (CPR), which I quoted toward the end of Chapter 2, demonstrates the tenor and effect of these debates on possible actions toward poverty. Once the problem of American poverty is named, the liberal CPR appeals to modern science to address the issues by reinvigorating the War on Poverty, employing research-based best practices that harness causal relationships in order to understand and end poverty. As Pinker suggested, the use of systematic evidence could discipline social actions in ways to reveal the mechanisms of poverty, its consequences, and its possible solutions. The CPR declares such action to be "sensible," but then, performs an immediate about-face to admit: "There are real political hurdles that make it difficult to take on poverty in any concerted way." Instead of insisting on actions that use reason to direct social policy to end poverty, CPR seeks to use science to "reduce the negative effects of poverty." Such is the current state of liberalism in America.

In this chapter, I examine what I mean as a liberal approach to reading education and poverty, explain philosophically why that connection is liberal, and review the history and effectiveness of several federal reading education interventions to address poverty over the past 50 years. The indefinite singular article before "a liberal approach" suggests that I see some unifying principles within liberalism. And I do, around definitions of equal opportunity, caring, rationality, government intervention, and progress. There are, I admit, a wide variety among liberal iterations of these principles within reading research and education communities.

Researchers and educators are vocal and voracious in their arguments about definitions, strategies, and outcomes toward those ends—and some might object to the "strange bedfellows" that I assign to a liberal category. That's why I take time to connect this approach to reading education to the moral, economic, and political goals of American liberalism—to demonstrate the overlap, if not overlay, of positions. I'll refer to various parts of the Elementary and Secondary Education Act (ESEA), originally passed in 1965, as a primary vehicle for federal intervention to protect the opportunities of poor children to take full advantage of the scientific reading instruction in public schools and preschools. From that base, CPR intends to pull interventions down toward infants and toddlers and push them out toward parents—all in the name of reducing poverty.

Liberal Reading Education
In the Community

In *Giving Our Children a Fighting Chance,* Susan Neuman and Donna Celano (2012) document two decades of their research on the relationships of poverty and literacy in some lives. They label their vantage point "the ecology of inequality," and work within and around two Philadelphia libraries where "the spatial concentration of poverty and affluence—in this case in the same school district—virtually guarantees the intergenerational transmission of class position" (p. 3). The authors chose the library because it symbolizes the United States' commitment to equality—the free and equal access to information and knowledge. Yet in vignette after vignette, as well as through systematic data analysis, Neuman and Celano show that the separation between poor and the rest of society creates practices and patterns "closely linked to one's education, and even more closely, with one's literacy skills" (p. 3), which largely direct one's life chances. Although others might interpret their results differently (see Cummins, 2007), Neuman and Celano provide an excellent liberal call for reading education to take the central place in efforts to reduce poverty in America.

Neuman and Celano work to overcome the "fundamental attribution error," a tendency to overemphasize individual factors and to underestimate contextual elements when probing the divergent outcomes between the well-to-do and poor. They begin by walking the neighborhoods surrounding the libraries to determine the physical presence of print in the two environments. Although the poor neighborhood had more signs, three quarters of those signs were in disrepair, while in the affluent neighborhood the signs were all in good condition. The affluent community afforded three times as many places to buy reading materials of any type and over 40 times as many titles. There were twice as many quality locations to read in this neighborhood, and the proprietors and managers seemed to welcome literate loiterers. Finished walking, Neuman and Celano concluded that the neighborhoods afford different opportunities to read print and that the gap established for young children widened throughout adolescence.

Once inside preschools, elementary schools, and libraries, Neuman and Celano expected to find a safety net of print to support the poor, and in fact, the gap in opportunities to read print did close somewhat. Preschool book collections were rated near excellent in the richer neighborhood and adequate in the poor. Directors mentioned differences in their abilities to maintain these collections. In the poor neighborhood, books were purchased with federal and state funds allotted in block grants with many competing priorities. The directors in the more affluent community explained that "the library" had a line item in their permanent budget. Within the elementary school libraries, the affluent schools had twice as many books per student that were in better shape and were tended by a licensed librarian. The libraries in the poor neighborhood showed the consequences of district budget cuts in which building principals diverted shrinking funds to other priorities. The volunteers and aides attempted to keep these libraries afloat. Neuman and Celano conclude that the access-to-print gap between the two groups continues when young children enter schools.

In the two libraries, Neuman and Celano found few differences between adult uses of the libraries: similar numbers of patrons, time reading, and preferences for nonfiction. From a distance, adolescents appeared to use the libraries in similar ways as well. Yet when the researchers approached the teen readers, they documented considerable difference between the complexities of the texts being read. In the poor library, teens were reading texts at grade level about 60 percent of the time and below grade level about 40 percent of the time. In the affluent library, teens read at grade level 93 percent of the time and above grade level the rest of the time they were observed. Similar disparities were noticed in children's and teens' uses of the technology available—in the wealthier neighborhood, the young spent greater percentages of their time surfing for information, and in the poorer neighborhood, young patrons' uses were more often classified as entertainment. Neuman and Celano imply that these literacy events are learned library behaviors and looked carefully at how adults in the library (parents and professionals) mediate children's time with text when at the library.

Because a local foundation provided a grant to "level the playing field" between the branches of the libraries, the physical condition of the interiors were comparable and access to technologies beyond the book collections were judged to be similar. The social demonstrations of library culture were quite distinct, however. In the poor neighborhood library, parents accompanied their children less often and rarely participated with their children when they were in attendance. Rather, for "story time" or selecting a book, children from the poor community attended as part of their preschool or daycare class. With less supervision, story times were less effective in providing book chats, good stories, or early literacy lessons. In contrast, children in the richer neighborhoods sat on their mothers' laps or by their sides as both adult and child participated in the librarian's activities and, then, wandered together discussing which books might be "just right" to take home or to discuss the uses of the Internet. Within these environments, the children formed different relationships with the librarians, developed different expectations of success for themselves within the environment, and acquired different library practices. Welcoming the foundation's generosity as goodhearted, Neuman and Celano conclude that the outcome of that project was much different than had been predicted. Rather than leveling the playing field, the children and the teens in the richer library used their learned library practices to increase their literate advantages in their communities.

For Neuman and Celano, poverty results from a lack of sufficient resources to sustain one's well-being. Through their research, they challenge the fundamental attribution error by showing how communities afford residents different opportunities to acquire economic capital through employment, social capital by networks beyond one's intimates, and cultural capital from negotiating effectively across institutions and powerful societal groups. The literate environments support the residents differently, making success much harder to achieve for the individuals in poor communities. Moreover, within the 21st-century global innovation economy, Neuman and Celano argue that informational capital is the most important resource to sustain oneself—"the cumulative product of a person's experiences with words and the concepts to which they refer" (p. 5) and logical, analytic reasoning. Their results suggest that the geographic isolation of poverty affords poor children fewer opportunities to acquire informational capital through direct experience, and per their results, less access to print and print-based practices that will extend their possibilities of accumulation of this capital. To prevent poverty, then, Neuman and Celano conclude that the poor must learn to read early and well in order to compensate for circumstances in which they were born, or at least, to have "a fighting chance" at a better life.

Other liberals have used research to identify these differences as well, not always, however, with the same sensitivity or epistemological assumptions. In fact, the original rationales for Head Start and Title 1 of the ESEA were based on the documentation of gaps in potentials and practices between poor and middle-class children. In *Poverty and Mental Retardation,* Rodger Hurley (1969) summarizes some of that documentation.

> The intellectual differences between a poor child and a middle-class child are not only caused by differences in the relative stability of their respective households. It is generally understood, although it has not been publicized, that there is a "hidden curriculum" in the middle class family, which virtually guarantees that the child will be more ready to begin school than his poor counterpart. The middle-class child is intensively tutored by his parents, especially his mother, and his rate of intellectual maturation is therefore

quicker. This training program was a part of the middle-class parents' own rearing pattern; because of the rewards and reinforcements they received from it, they pass the same training on to their children. (pp. 78–79)

In *Ways With Words* Shirley Brice Heath (1983) frames these differences as discourses, various ways of using language, time, space, and story without affixing Hurley's implied value judgment. The poor African American and White working-class families in her study had completely functional ways with words within their communities, but those ways didn't always travel well across other communities or easily to schools. In contrast, Black and White townsfolk had acquired multiple ways with words for different contexts through experiences and teaching, and these ways were closer to the expectations at school. James Gee (1992) wrote: "Let us call discourses that lead to social goods in a society 'dominant discourses' and let us refer to those groups that have the fewest conflicts when using them as 'dominant groups' " (p. 24). Failure to master dominant discourses limits individuals' life chances. And later, Gee (2008) asks: "Have all children in a given learning environment had equal opportunity to learn the specialist forms of language vital for thought and action in the domain they are seeking to learn?" (p. 100).

Neuman and Celano answer "no," and offer nuanced explanations of what could be done in poor neighborhoods to prepare residents for the demands of the 21st century. In order to overcome the print and information handicap, poor children and adolescents need more access to smart tools (print, digital, and visual texts) to be sure, but more importantly, more effective mediation of their use of these tools. Training is essential—parents and mentors to help preschoolers negotiate the print in their environments directly, librarians and volunteers to assist poor children and teens with choices and uses of media, and preschool and elementary teachers to engage students' minds in ways that help them to answer the question "what is reading for?" Each and all of these steps would increase the distribution of information capital within poor communities, leading eventually to accumulation of cultural, social, and economic capital.

In a postscript, Neuman and Celano move beyond their data to take a pragmatic look at school reform. They chide politicians, pundits, and educators who propose "the magic bullet" or "miracle" in order to describe the hard work of increasing the informational capital of all children and youth, but most particularly, among the poor. Acknowledging that schools can be intellectual wastelands, they celebrate the results of a continuum of models for schooling. Their personal preference, they admit, would be the curriculum and pedagogy practice at the Urban Academy, an inquiry-based program based on the expectation that poor teens are interested and capable of asking and addressing "hard questions," using dominant discourses as well as disrupting those discourses with alternative ones. Their last words are saved for the successes of what they label "paternalistic schools," highly prescriptive institutions that teach students not just how to think but also how to act according to middle-class values (e.g., Knowledge is Power Program [KIPP], Excellence, and even Core Knowledge). Simply, they state: "it's not about us . . . they serve students well" (p. 141).

In Schools

Anthony Bryk and his colleagues (2010) were members of The Consortium on Chicago School Research when they conducted a longitudinal study of the effects of the Chicago School Reform Act from the governor's signing in 1988 until Mayor Daley's takeover of city schools in 1995. The Act granted decentralized authority to local councils in 575 individual schools across the city in order to improve student learning. Over the previous 20 years, Chicago had lost over 300,000 manufacturing jobs, neighborhoods had become more segregated by race and class, and as a consequence, schools were segregated by race and class (80 percent American students attended nearly all-Black schools, 40 percent ilies lived below the poverty line, and 82 percent of students were nd reduced lunch). At the time the Act passed, dropout rates were ievement was low, and leadership was unstable. In 1988 Secretary lliam Bennett labeled Chicago Public Schools "the worst in the

he Act, community members would elect a council (two teachd two local community members) who would consult with and ipal when making personnel decisions, developing an annual budget, and negotiating the school's improvement plan. In order to support the decentralization of authority, the Act allotted $500,000 in discretionary funds for each school to be distributed across the first five years of transition. These funds could be used for hiring additional staff; purchasing new equipment, materials, and programs; and securing professional development for employees. Councils were able to select and evaluate the principal based on criteria established in the improvement plan, and in exchange for losing tenure security, building principals gained the right to make personnel decisions without union interference and to design the school improvement plan and budget. Bryk and his colleagues (2010) considered the Act the context for a natural experiment.

> We strive to understand the internal workings and external conditions that distinguish improving elementary schools from those that fail to do so. In so doing, we aim to establish a comprehensive empirically grounded theory of practice—in this instance, the practice of organizing schools for improvements—that teachers, parents, principals, superintendents, and civic leaders can draw on as they work to improve children's learning in thousands of schools all across this land. (p.11)

In preliminary work, Bryk and his associates (2010) established that structural change happened during two phases. First, "creative chaos" challenged the dysfunctional status quo in elementary schools, and then in some schools, change took hold. Their data told the story of three thirds, in which one third of Chicago's elementary schools engaged in self-activating restructuring; a second third accepted the challenge but were struggling to maintain; and the last third demonstrated few signs of change at all. "Of significance, successful reform initiation had occurred across a broad cross section of communities, largely without regard to class or race" (p. 17). Yet, schools in the final third had predominantly African American enrollments with 90 percent of the students from very low-income families. To develop a school improvement model, Bryk and his colleagues compared the conditions between elementary schools in which change crystallized and sustained and those most resistant to change.

In order to examine the reform's impacts on attendance, reading, and mathematics, Bryk and the others constructed two measures that enabled them to control enrollment transience and captured the school's contribution to students' scores on the Iowa Test of Basic Skills. Based on their early study in these schools, the researchers hypothesized four essential supports for change:

1. Professional capacity (i.e., teacher's knowledge and skills, professional development, and professional community);
2. School learning climate (i.e., teachers' expectations, order and safety, and peer relationships);
3. Parent, school, and community ties (i.e., community social services, parental support for school, and school's efforts to engage parents);
4. Instructional guidance (i.e., curricular alignment, support for curricular decisions, and pedagogical emphasis).

Bryk and others added school leadership as a fifth dimension for their hypothesized model of school change when they noted that some principals and district consultants were more inclusive than others of teachers, local school councils, and community members in their work around the school improvement plan.

Through elaborate statistics, inventive charts, and careful prose, the researchers demonstrate that the five hypothesized elements were indeed supports, essential and connected to each other in a framework. Schools strong in most supports were at least 10 times more likely to show substantial gains in reading achievement scores. After a dip in scores during the initial transition, schools with high evidence of change toward the coordinated establishment of these essential supports demonstrated a steady climb from 22 percent reaching or exceeding national norms in 1990 to 37 percent in 1996. Without these essential supports, scores remained flat. The most successful schools used ongoing professional development to improve teachers' knowledge and pedagogy. When coupled with a supportive work environment and an inclusive leader who brokered consensus on a common, coherent, and aligned instructional system, student gains were larger. The largest gains were demonstrated when these elements were supported by solid parent and community ties with faculty and staff. Bryk and his colleagues report: "While in retrospect this may all seem rather straightforward and easy to summarize, establishing the empirical warrant for these conclusions has been far from simple" (p. 126).

Two surprises were found. First, schools employed a variety of approaches to reading instruction without direct correlation to success. Teachers used didactic and project-based pedagogies in successful and unsuccessful schools. Regardless of the approach, students scored higher on tests when teachers aligned the reading curriculum and pedagogy across grade levels. However, Bryk and colleagues report that didactic instruction on isolated basic skills appeared "dull and repetitious," leading students away from active engagement, while "constructivist" pedagogy led to more interest and higher attendance. To a degree, this finding confirms Neuman and Celano's conclusion that both inquiry-based and paternalistic school programs can be successful in low-income communities, adding data to support their personal preferences.

Second, in 10 percent of Chicago schools, Bryk and colleagues found very high levels of racial and income segregation—over 95 percent racial minority enrollment and yearly median family incomes below $9,500. In these schools, attempts to change school programs were seldom effective, and none were sustained over the seven years of the study. Regardless of what initial approach was taken, students' reading achievement test scores flatlined. Bryk and his colleagues call for studies that treat race and income as more than demographic descriptors in order to determine how the segregated nature of such communities stymies academic change and achievement. Similar to other liberals (e.g., Berliner, 2009; Rothstein, 2004), they hypothesize that out-of-school antipoverty interventions would be necessary to improve "true disadvantaged" students' reading achievement, and they seek empirical warrants to support these claims.

Brighouse and Schouten (2011) take up Bryk and colleagues' challenge, reviewing research literature associated with student achievement in low-income communities. Although they find mixed empirical results for in-school interventions concerning low-income students' achievement, they note the continued political commitment of pundits, government officials, and foundations to charter schools, longer school days, stringent disciplinary norms, and rigorous back-to-basics curricula organized in "high commitment" schools (Neuman and Celano's paternalistic schools). As a result, researchers studying in-school factors find it easier to obtain funding for their studies and more outlets for dissemination. Brighouse and Schouten identify only the Broader, Bolder Approach to Education (BBA) coalition as a primary source for longitudinal studies of out-of-school interventions of income, segregation, and health care. For example BBA researchers Wise and Long (2013) concluded that urban schools that coordinated in-school effort with community health care agencies produced higher achievement among low-income students than urban schools with in-school interventions alone. The BBA titled the Wise and Long report *Market Oriented Education Reforms' Rhetoric Trumps Reality*.

In the Classroom

Liberal reading education is predicated on the notion that every student should have an equal opportunity to learn to read. Attempts to compensate for fewer resources available in poor communities are expected to level the amounts of social, cultural, and informational capital that students bring to school each day. Essential supports within schools are intended to create and maintain that balance while all students learn to read in an acceptable manner to, at least, a predetermined degree. If successful, then differences in students' reading achievement would be due only to personal capabilities and investments and not because of systemic social biases and economic inequalities. Because all community and school interventions are works in progress, this liberal challenge enters every public school classroom daily.

Over the last half century, much of the work in reading education has intended to identify, organize, and supply the best tools, practices, dispositions, and knowledge in order to meet that challenge. Since the beginning, however, workers in that field—both teachers and researchers—have struggled over the criteria to determine what "best" means. These debates took place and continue to take place on ontological and epistemological grounds concerning fundamental questions: What is reading? How does it happen? When and why is it learned? and How do we know if someone is reading? In fact, the field of reading education emerged when individuals began to apply scientific rationality to traditional answers to these questions over 100 years ago (Shannon, 2007). Educational psychologist Edmund Burke Huey (1908/1968) captured this agenda in one brief statement: "After all we have thus far been content with trial and error, too often allowing publishers to be our jury, and a real rationalization of the process of inducing the child with the practice of reading has not been made" (p. 9).

While liberals agreed that a "real rationalization" of reading education pedagogy was needed if progress was to be made in developing a literate populace, they did not agree on the type of rationality that should direct this action. To be sure, over the last century the experimental search for one best method has dominated the field of reading research through the identification and testing of the psychological processes of reading and instruction. Yet consistent across that time, others have pursued different notions of scientific rationality—ones based on social and cultural interpretation of reading and reading education. When William S. Gray was summarizing the psychological studies of reading and teaching in the 1920s for The National Society for the Study of Education, Carolyn Pratt was watching her students at the City and Country School represent their lives through multimodal systems—toys, blocks, paint, and print. In the 1960s, while Jeanne S. Chall was adjudicating the great debate over beginning reading instruction through a summary of 67 studies for the National Conference of Research in English,

Kenneth Goodman was interpreting children's oral reading miscues as their strategic use of their life experiences with language and the world to negotiate meaning. In the 1980s, as Richard C. Anderson and others were summarizing the "state of art" of reading research for the National Academy of Education, Jerome Harste, Virginia Woodward, and Carolyn Burke were explaining literacy lessons from the language stories they gathered while observing the literate "lived through experiences" of preschoolers. All claimed rightfully their findings to be scientific.

These tensions are still apparent within the liberal position on classroom reading instruction for low-income students. For example, Louisa Moats (2008) summarized cognitive research in order to argue for direct, explicit, intense, and targeted reading instruction in schools serving the poor. According to her review, all low-income students must follow the same curriculum, beginning with phonological awareness, proceeding through fluent application of phonic knowledge, and leading to word recognition, word meaning, and passage comprehension. Although children from wealthier neighborhoods might be able to compensate for deviations from this path, Moats cites research to report that poor children rarely "catch up" on their own. Because fidelity to this sequence is vital, she recommends instructional scripts that standardized content, pace, and delivery of instruction in order to equalize all students' opportunities to learn to read.

Kathryn Au (2011) looks at the same research and places these cognitive functions of reading within social and cultural contexts. From her vantage point, equal opportunities to learn to read require teachers' sensitivity to diversity among students' ways with words and the funds of knowledge that they bring to the classroom each day. Although a teacher's goals remain the same for all students, one preplanned curriculum and one style of pedagogy cannot afford all students equal opportunities due to these differences. Au bases her conclusions on decades of work with school districts serving diverse populations, and she offers four "proven effective keys to success" in closing the racial and income reading achievement gaps: recognizing the solution must be multifaceted, building instruction around higher-level thinking with text, working from the language and knowledge that students bring to school, and fostering collaboration among teachers with a shared vision of reading as a social practice.

Despite obvious differences, Moats and Au share liberal values concerning poverty. They begin with the assumption that the government is responsible for protecting the equal rights of all citizens and, therefore, public schools should provide equal opportunities for all students to prepare themselves to live productive lives. They empathize with those who currently suffer the consequences of poverty and note that schools could and should ameliorate future consequences through effective and efficient reading instruction for low-income students. Both assume that learning to read will enable low-income students to take advantage of more opportunities to make a sustainable living through participation in the economy and civic life. They acknowledge, however, that currently the income achievement gap is increasing and call for direct intervention, using science as the means to determine the best solution to that problem. They expect their scientific rationality to displace tradition, prestige, and even common sense in reading education in order to fulfill the liberal promise of equality. Similar to the reading researchers across the 20th century, only their definitions and approaches to science differ.

In *An Elusive Science: The Troubling History of Education Research,* Ellen Condliffe Lagemann (2000) explains how this lack of consensus about educational science has stymied liberals' agenda for progress in public schools. An inability or unwillingness to agree on a common epistemology and a common ontology has blocked educational researchers from engaging in conduct of normal science that has proved to be productive in engineering and medicine. In those fields, researchers were and are mentored toward agreement on best practices and values, allowing studies to build consistently on one another and leading systemically toward measureable goals. In this way, policy makers and the public have clear criteria on which to judge the importance and utility of any finding. Within educational research, these criteria remain the subject of vigorous debate, leading Lagemann to draw a remarkably similar conclusion to that which Huey stated nearly a century earlier.

> It is startling to discover just how few regulations exist in education. It is similarly amazing to realize that publishers, test makers, and reformers of every color and stripe can "sell" their wares without prior piloting or evaluation. . . . In consequence, successful innovations in education are more dependent on entrepreneurship than on the validity of the research that supports them. (Lagemann, 2000, p. 238)

Liberal Reading Education Policy

Liberals take a pragmatic approach to policy. They name a problem, define a desired goal, and then search for a solution to address, if not solve, the problem. Because liberals assume that human intelligence can make sense of the natural and social world, they propose and enact policies of intervention and regulation, believing that the outcomes will be predictable across geographic and cultural scales. To evaluate the success of a policy, outcomes are measured across time against the desired goals. If a policy does not help individuals and institutions make progress toward the goal, then the policy should be withdrawn (think early American poor laws in which debt meant prison, therefore criminalizing poverty). Some or much progress toward the goals means continuation with adjustments along the way (Medicare has improved the health of the elderly). Few policies achieve their goals completely. And there are always unanticipated consequences even within highly successful programs (the Supplemental Nutrition Assistance Program kept many families from poverty during the Great Recession, but the eligibility cards have become a form of currency for desperately poor individuals after their Temporary Assistance for Needy Families and/or workman's compensation have ended [Deparle & Gebeloff, 2010]).

Larry Cuban (2010) explains that policy making is not just a rational process. To begin, policy makers and their associates (this can be a large group—from concerned citizens to support staff to lobbyists and paid consultants of all stripes) struggle to name the problem and to propose possible solutions. Before policy makers try any, they compare and contrast the potential of these alternatives in terms of probable cost and benefits until they decide on which one is most likely to achieve the goal(s) and test it in the real world. As Cuban (2010) states: "A policy is both a hypothesis and argument that a particular action should be taken to solve a problem. That action, however, has to be politically acceptable and economically feasible." This reality can be frustrating to liberal reading researchers who assume that policy makers should always defer to scientific authority when making decisions (see, for example, "Ideology Still Trumping Evidence," in Allington, 2002).

The Elementary and Secondary Education Act

Congress enacted the Elementary and Secondary Education Act on April 11, 1965, as part of the War on Poverty portion of President Johnson's Great Society legislative agenda. The bill passed through Congress in only 87 days with little debate and no amendments proposed from the floor. Its original purpose was straightforward with few strings attached.

> In recognition of the special educational needs of low-income families and the impact that concentrations of low-income families have on the ability of local educational agencies to support adequate educational programs, the Congress hereby declares it to be the policy of the United States to provide assistance . . . to local educational agencies serving areas with concentrations of children from low-income families to expand and improve their educational programs by various means (including preschool programs) which contribute to meeting the special educational needs of educationally deprived children. (Elementary and Secondary Education Act, 1965, Section 201)

Title 1 of ESEA was/is intended to enable states to provide compensatory instruction for poor students, distributing one billion dollars annually among schools willing to participate.

Although the public debate about ESEA was quiet, legislators negotiated the particulars of the new law. According to McLaughlin (1975), Senator Robert Kennedy doubted school officials' sincerity for teaching the poor and argued for accountability systems in which schools reported periodically to the parents of disadvantaged children. For Kennedy, Title 1 was to be a service program ensuring equal access to good instruction. Unless school officials were required to report, he believed that school officials would accept the federal funding but spend it according to established local priorities and not the federal ones. Education Commissioner Francis Keppel accepted the need for program evaluation and an accountability system, but thought they would enable state and federal officials to compare school performances and, therefore, healthy competition would stimulate movement toward more efficient and effective instruction for the poor.

The new federal office of Program Evaluation within the Department of Health, Education, and Welfare accepted Keppel's interpretation and proposed that the Planning, Programming, and Budgeting System (PPBS) be used to develop clear specific Title 1 goals, precise measurements, and explicit criteria for cost/benefit analysis. The recommendation changed the purpose of evaluation and reporting from Kennedy's recommendation—to make low-income parents partners in Title 1 services—to a means by which state and federal officials could identify the most efficient and effective approaches for educating disadvantaged students. In this new marketplace of ideas, the liberal officials assumed that school personnel would gravitate toward the best practices, allowing the Title 1 funds to get "the most bang for its buck."

Fearing that an evaluation system would usurp states' rights to govern schools, leading to a federal takeover of public schooling, many state and school officials negotiated an explicit statement within ESEA barring those possibilities. The federal government could not "exercise any direction, supervision, or control over the curriculum, program of instruction, administration or personnel, or over the selection of any instructional materials in any educational institution or school system" (Public Law 89–10, Section 604). With that declaration in place, in 1965 Title 1 became the first large-scale social program requiring a formal evaluation. However, in the original wording for the evaluation there were no uniform reporting procedures, requirements for specific standardized tests, or consequences for noncompliance. School officials would report to parents as they deemed appropriate and local districts would provide descriptions of Title 1 services to the state, which in turn would report on general state trends to the federal agency. According to House (1978), these initial reports revealed little beyond the fact that district officials appreciated the increased funding and the claim that low-income students had greater access to educational opportunities.

These reports frustrated both Kennedy's concern for political accountability to poor parents and the Office of Education's interest in finding the most efficient means to raise achievement. After two years, Title 1 evaluations became more closely tied to standardized tests administered according to federal guidelines. With this new tool, federal officials assumed that Title 1 effects could be identified, tied to background variables, and assembled into a model representing the most efficient teaching methods. General Electric was hired to conduct the first evaluation (named TEMPO) on a select group of Title 1 programs in large cities. After considerable expense, however, the study failed to identify achievement gains in reading among Title 1 students. The lack of uniformity among Title 1 within and across school districts precluded valid and reliable statistical comparisons. Congressional opponents of ESEA used TEMPO results to freeze Title 1 funding at its original level.

The Office of Education argued that TEMPO had revealed that state and local control of Title 1 programs foiled any efforts to identify successes or failures, and proposed a planned variation model for Title 1 programs evaluation. Competing hypotheses about teaching the poor would be operationalized into clearly delineated programs that could be implemented with fidelity in order to allow the formal PPBS evaluation system to work. With this approach, the federal government assumed more control over Title 1 program inputs and design as well as the evaluation of state and local services. Planned variation evaluation began with Project Follow Through in the 1970s (a project that followed Head Start students through the primary grades), which ended decades-long arguments over the definition and merits of the goals, measures, or results (see Englemann, 1992; House, Glass, McLean, & Walker, 1978; Lagemann, 2000). Attempts to design Title 1 PPBS program evaluation systems have continued over the last 50 years (see Bryk et al., 2010).

In 1968, however, in order to provide Education Commissioner Harold Howe with data that he could take to Congress to argue for the continuation of Title 1 funding, Office of Education officials deviated from the PPBS strategy, conducting "quick" national surveys of Title 1 programs believed to be successful (Hawkridge, Albert, Chalupsky, & Roberts, 1968). Rather than an accounting of results to parents or a means to identify the one best system, these actions sought simply to describe existing programs and to identify "what was working" in some programs at that time. Named the "It Works" project, the case studies established what Bryk et al. (2010) might call four "straightforward and easy" conclusions, but without empirical warrants. The "stories" from the cases proved to be successful with Congress.

> Good program design and effective guidelines establishing criteria were crucial to effecting program evaluation.
>
> Successful preschool programs all had certain common attributes: careful planning, including statement of objectives; teacher training in the methods of the program; small groups, allowing a high degree of individualization; and instruction and materials closely aligned with the objectives.
>
> Successful compensatory education at the elementary level largely depended upon: academic objectives clearly stated, active parental involvement particularly as motivation, individual attention for pupils' learning problems and a high intensity of treatment.
>
> Successful compensatory programs in large numbers focused on the provision of remedial reading services for elementary school students. (McLaughlin, 1975, p. 83)

Compensatory Reading Education Policy

The Educational Testing Service completed the survey of Title 1 compensatory instruction in 1971, and a committee from the International Reading Association (IRA) performed a second analysis on the data describing reading education (Calfee & Drum, 1979). The survey sampled over 14,000 school districts that received Title 1 funding. Generally, results showed that the number of students with reading difficulties increased across primary into intermediate grades as the text demands increased, however, in wealthier schools with higher rates of per-pupil funding, fewer students experienced reading difficulties in either primary or intermediate grades. Although principals and compensatory teachers reported general satisfaction with the infrastructure for their Title 1 programs, the IRA committee was concerned about the lack of appropriate preparation among compensatory teachers and the absence of certified reading specialists in two thirds of the schools. For example, only 25 percent of the compensatory teachers met the IRA professional standards for teachers of reading, and 69 percent lacked even a single course in the "assessment and correction" of reading difficulties.

Most troubling to the IRA committee was the finding that few students "graduated" from Title 1 programs because their reading became commensurate with that of their peers. The committee blamed teachers' dispositions and program design. Although most teachers responded that it was theoretically possible for slower students to improve their reading abilities with extra instruction, 60 percent doubted that their Title 1 students possessed sufficient verbal abilities, cognitive attributes, and stable self-concepts to enable them to take advantage of the opportunities made available through Title 1 programs. On average, teachers devoted only 30 minutes a day to reading instruction. Primary students received more instructional time despite the fact that the number of students with reading difficulties increased across grades. In two-thirds of the programs, compensatory instruction supplanted regular instruction rather than augmented it as required. The IRA committee found few differences between regular and compensatory reading instruction because nearly all elementary teachers (regular and compensatory) followed a regular regime prescribed in the teachers manuals from commercially prepared materials, substituting workbook and worksheet practice of basic subskills for direct teaching of comprehension strategies and extended time reading books at appropriate grade levels.

Since the 1970s liberal policies for compensatory reading instruction have emerged from negotiations of tensions found in these early evaluative studies of Title 1 and ESEA: the assumption, but absence, of rational decision making about reading instruction among school personnel; the continuous pursuit of more scientific warrants to guide those decisions; and pragmatic experimentation in order to discover effective incentives to encourage rational decision making in states, schools, and classrooms based on those warrants. (As I'll take up in Chapters 4 and 5, conservatives and neoliberals also participated in these negotiations.) The results of those negotiations can be found in the Bush Administration's reauthorization of the ESEA—the No Child Left Behind (NCLB) Act of 2001. After 40 years of arguing over the goals and implementation of ESEA, the 2001 Statement of Purpose for Title 1 conveys some liberal frustration.

> The purpose of this title is to ensure that all children have a fair, equal, and significant opportunity to obtain a high-quality education and reach, at a minimum, proficiency on challenging State academic achievement standards and state academic assessments. This purpose can be accomplished by:
>
> (1) ensuring that high-quality academic assessments, accountability systems, teacher preparation and training, curriculum, and instructional materials are aligned with challenging State academic standards so that students, teachers, parents, and administrators can measure progress against common expectations for student academic achievement;
> (2) meeting the educational needs of low achieving children in our Nation's highest poverty schools, limited English proficient children, migratory children, children with disabilities, Indian children, neglected and delinquent children, and young children in need of reading assistance; . . .
> (4) holding schools, local educational agencies, and States accountable for improving the academic achievement of all students, and identifying and turning around low performing schools that have failed to provide a high quality education to their students, while providing alternatives to students in such schools to enable the students to receive a high quality education; . . .
> (9) promoting schoolwide reform and ensuring the access of children to effective, scientifically based instructional strategies and challenging academic content; . . .
> (10) significantly elevating the quality of instruction by providing staff in participating schools with substantial opportunities for professional development; . . . (Title 1: Sec. 1001)

Rather than simply sending funding to states in order to provoke equal opportunities for low-income students as states and school personnel saw fit, NCLB required student proficiency on challenging academic standards as measured by state exams with the expectation that all students would make annual progress toward universal proficiency in 2014. While this system has the potential to identify the most efficient programs through PPBS procedures, the Title I Statement of Purpose directs attention to identifying and correcting low-performing schools. Through professional development and the coordination of services, NCLB assumes that all teachers would provide scientifically based instruction coordinated to promote school-wide reform and universal proficiency. With increased,

48 Opportunity

but enlightened, federal intervention, officials assumed the goals of ESEA would finally be met by 2014.

For liberals, the justification for increased federal intervention rested on the science behind the actions. Progress toward the scientific understanding of reading and the teaching of reading warranted the centralization of rational decision making at the federal level in order to ensure equal opportunity to learn to read across all the states. Between 1979 and 2001 reading research had increased dramatically, bolstering liberal confidence that interventions, if handled correctly, could achieve equal opportunities for all American students to learn to read. However, liberals could not reach consensus about what constitutes reading, science, or progress. Compare, for example, the following two comments.

> Historically, public abhorrence of unpreparedness has triggered a metamorphosis in numerous professions: medicine, pharmacology, accounting, actuarial sciences and seafaring. . . . The metamorphosis results in movement toward a mature profession. This postmetamorphosis state is characterized by the increasing use of scientific methods for determining efficacy: a) a shift from judgment of individual experts to judgments constrained by quantified data that can be inspected by a broad audience, b) less emphasis on personal trust and more emphasis on objectivity, and c) diminished autonomy by experts and a greater role for standardized measures and procedures informed by scientific investigation. Education is just beginning to go through a metamorphosis from an immature to a mature profession. (Carnine, 1999, p. 2)

> I contend that education, including the teaching of reading, is more like fostering healthy human development, building a successful business, maintaining an effective military and providing good parenting than it is like administering medical or psychological interventions. American business and the American military are each the envy of the world, yet imagine how little of their cumulative wisdom and common practice are supported by the kind of research the NRP would insist upon for investigating claims about reading instruction. For instance, what would happen if parents began to feel doubts about any practice that does not have enough experimental support to conduct a meta-analysis? (Cunningham, 2001, p. 326)

Between the publication of these statements, the National Institute of Child Health and Human Development published the *Teaching Children to Read* report (National Reading Panel, 2000), which was intended to establish scientifically based reading instruction. The National Reading Panel (NRP) summarized existing knowledge about reading and reading instruction according to strict experimentalist and statistical criteria. The NRP members positioned previous federally funded syntheses of reading research—*Becoming a Nation of Readers* (Anderson, Hiebert, Scott, &

Wilkerson, 1985), *Beginning to Read* (Adams, 1990), and *Preventing Reading Difficulties in Young Children* (Snow, Burns, & Griffin, 1998)—as subjective because each had relied on achieving consensus among experts and not on an objective statistical process. Accordingly, the NRP members excluded considerable bodies of historical, phenomenological, ethnographic, critical, post-structural, and pragmatic reading research from consideration in their synthesis. Using its experimentalist criteria, the NRP report sanctioned a psychological stage model of learning to read in which mastery of phonemic awareness and fluent application of phonic knowledge preceded word, and then, text comprehension. With the publication of the NRP, and its subsequent connection to NCLB in 2001, federal authorities established the official definition of scientifically based reading curriculum and instruction and prescribed them for all schools receiving federal funding.

In order to facilitate schools' progress toward meeting that mandate, Congress built the Reading First Initiative according to the NRP model. It was designed to be a whole school supplement to Title 1 to launch all students toward reading proficiency across their school careers. Congress allocated nine million dollars annually to support the initial five years of the initiative. Reading First was intended to:

1. To provide assistance to State educational agencies and local educational agencies in establishing reading programs for students in kindergarten through grade 3 that are based on scientifically based reading research, to ensure that every student can read at grade level or above not later than the end of grade 3.
2. To provide assistance to State educational agencies and local educational agencies in preparing teachers, including special education teachers, through professional development and other support, so the teachers can identify specific reading barriers facing their students and so the teachers have the tools to effectively help their students learn to read.
3. To provide assistance to State educational agencies and local educational agencies in selecting or administering screening, diagnostic, and classroom-based instructional reading assessments.
4. To provide assistance to State educational agencies and local educational agencies in selecting or developing effective instructional materials (including classroom-based materials to assist teachers in implementing the essential components of reading instruction), programs, learning systems, and strategies to implement methods that have been proven to prevent or remediate reading failure within a State.
5. To strengthen coordination among schools, early literacy programs, and family literacy programs to improve reading achievement for all children. (Subpart 1: Reading First, Section 1201)

With the Reading First Initiative within NCLB, federal officials believed they had finally found the most efficient program for teaching low-income (and all) students to read. In order to ensure that local programs would follow scientifically based practices for all students, Reading First required the disaggregation of standards-based state test scores by demographic category (race, social class, home language, and disability). The fact that states proposed the standards and commissioned the tests kept the original ESEA promise to abstain from national standards. However, state officials were to submit their expected standards and their tests to federal authorities for approval, and this added a layer of federal quality control. For the evaluation process, districts would first submit their designs to state officials, who would evaluate them based on scientific evidence. Once approved, districts would describe the rate at which they would ensure students' progress toward universal proficiency in 2014. This rate of annual progress would be the criterion with which each school's effectiveness would be evaluated. Schools that faltered would suffer penalties. Additionally, district proposals were to explain how they would make use of national networks of federally funded intermediate units designed to support and monitor Reading First progress. With this level of oversight concerning standards, goals, materials, and plans, ESEA officials were confident that after more than 35 years, they finally had achieved a balance between incentives and mandates to ensure that school officials and teachers act rationally toward low-income students. In order to identify the best programs, federal officials insisted that each state participate in the National Assessment of Educational Progress (NAEP) examination—the national report card.

Working from the summary of the NRP, all states eventually produced acceptable proposals for state standards and received Reading First Initiative funding. Although federal officials would later deny that they promoted any particular form of reading instruction, most state and school officials recognized that districts were expected to adopt a commercial core reading program and to implement plans for scientifically based professional development in order to ensure that teachers would implement that program properly. To leave little to chance, federal officials provided a list of core reading programs that it argued fit the official specifications (e.g., Open Court Reading, Mastery Reading, Harcourt, Houghton Mifflin, and Scott Foresman), and they set official guidelines for acceptable fundable professional development. At least in Pennsylvania, if a district submitted an unacceptable proposal, state officials assigned technical advisors to encourage the districts to adopt an acceptable core reading program, specific commercial achievement tests, and a single approved provider of professional development. Eventually, all districts developed accepted proposals.

The Department of Education Office of Planning, Evaluation, and Policy Development conducted the Reading First Implementation Study in 2008–2009. The study compared a stratified sample of classrooms that employed Reading First criteria with Title 1 programs from schools without the Reading First program, and it also compared Reading First schools with matched non–Reading First schools. The implementation evaluation survey reported that Reading First schools had reading coaches to assist teachers in delivering the program, reading materials aligned with scientifically based reading research, used assessment to guide instruction, placed struggling readers in intervention programs, and had teachers participate in professional development programs based on the NRP report. The Reading First Implementation Study was designed to assess the impact of the program on classroom instruction and student reading achievement. Based on direct observations in Grades 1 and 2 classrooms, the study concluded that Reading First teachers spent significantly more time on the five components recommended in the NRP report, but "found no evidence that Reading First had a statistically significant impact on student reading comprehension test scores in grades 1, 2, or 3 across the three years of the study" (Gamse et al., 2011, p. 2). After a conflict-of-interest controversy over federal advocacy of materials, tests, and professional development services and the impact evaluations, Congress cut the Reading First funding—first by 60 percent in 2007, and then completely in 2009.

The NAEP examinations also revealed problems with NCLB's approach to helping low-income students learn to read. Although President Bush pointed to rising state test scores throughout his two administrations as evidence that Reading First was working, Jaekyung Lee (2006) from the Harvard Civil Rights Project found neither a significant rise in achievement scores nor reductions in the racial or income achievement gaps. For example, Lee reported at the rate of growth in achievement celebrated by the Bush Administration, only 34 percent of all American students and only 24 percent of low-income students would become proficient readers by the 2014 target date. Moreover, Lee identified significant gaps between the number of students achieving proficiency on state tests and those rated as proficient on the NAEP exam. For example, Alabama reported 83 percent proficiency among students on the state exam, but NAEP reported only 22 percent proficiency for Alabama students. Similar discrepancies were found in all states (e.g., 82 percent to 37 percent in New Jersey and 81 percent to 29 percent in Oregon). While state officials' claims were twice as likely to inflate scores for White and middle-class students, they were four times more likely to overstate proficiency rates among poor and minority students, therefore, denying them the needed compensatory reading instruction.

Learning from the demise of the Reading First Initiative and NCLB's attempt to standardize the implementation of the NRP report, liberals moved in two policy directions. First, many recognized the need to contextualize the NRP report within social and cultural research it had excluded. Apparently, there could be different routes, to paraphrase Huey from 1908, of "inducing" different children with the practices of reading. Neuman and Celano's and Au's books embrace and demonstrate this move; both echo Bryk and others' findings that essential supports for reading instruction require both faculty and community commitment to and participation in any plans to improve reading instruction. Acknowledging that needed support extends well beyond decoding in the primary grades, many liberals embraced the common core standards movement and its not so subtle shift in priorities from initial interpretations of the NRP (phonemic awareness, phonics, and fluency fast and furious) to an emphasis on vocabulary and comprehension instruction across the grades and academic disciplines (Neuman & Gambrell, 2013). This shift deepened the model operationalized in public schools and more closely approximated the recommendations of the 2002 RAND Corporation's *Reading for Understanding* report (Snow, 2002) and the model of reading tested during NAEP examinations (Pearson, 2013). To bring these new priorities to the classroom, teachers must retool accordingly. Although debates continue around the efficiency and effectiveness of tightly aligned systems from standards to instruction through testing, a liberal consensus formed around both positions as the rational decision to make given the evidence.

Second, despite all efforts since the original ESEA, liberals recognized that low-income children still do not enter school well prepared to take advantage of what schools offer (Issacs, 2012). Reardon's (2011) research identified that over the last 30 years this disparity has become a three-part divide with nearly identical gaps between rich and middle-class students and, then, between middle and low-income students. Low-income children lag 12–14 months behind the norms of their middle-class peers in both language development and pre-reading skills (Barnett, Carolan, Fitzgerald, & Squires, 2013), and, as Neuman and Celano (2012) demonstrated, they are even further behind in the acquisition of informational capital. While these gaps do widen after students enter school, Reardon pointed out that schooling accounts for only 10 percent of the gap by high school. Although he acknowledges that income segregation contributes to the gap before and during school, he argues that well-to-do parents now invest more capital directly into their children's preschool cognitive development and cultural capital. Echoing the recommendations of the Collaboration for Poverty Research, liberals call for scientifically based preschool programs for low-income children directed at enhancing their cognitive and language development as well as parent education and even intervention into low-income homes in order to make equal opportunity to learn to read at school even a possibility for low-income children.

Yet in their *State of Preschool 2012 Yearbook,* the National Institute for Early Education Research (NIEER) reported that states have backed away from investing in young children (Barnett et al., 2013). Over the last decade, state funding for preschool programs declined by $400 per child. This reduction influenced both the quality of the programs and size of preschool enrollments. Less than 25 percent of the programs met all 10 of NIEER standards for quality preschool programs. Two-thirds of teaching faculties did not have the recommended academic qualifications, and the same number of programs lacked regular oversight from sponsoring agencies. Less than half offered a recommended academic curriculum with explicit goals for language and cognitive development. And only half kept enrollments below the recommended 20 children per class or had the 10:1 children-to-faculty ratio as recommended. Only a third was able to offer screening low-income children for vision, dental, or health concerns. One quarter offered at least one meal per day. In 2012 state-funded programs enrolled only 4 percent of eligible three-year-olds and 28 percent of four-year-olds. When the federally funded Head Start enrollments were added, 14 percent of three-year-olds and 41 percent of four-year-olds participated in public preschool programs.

Liberals understand poverty as a lack of resources to sustain one's family or oneself. Their lack of resources is a consequence of systematic inequalities in individuals' and groups' opportunities to take advantage of the institutions designed to support human development and self-sufficiency. Liberals believe governments to be primarily responsible to ensure equal opportunity and, therefore, government officials have the right, and the duty, to intervene when inequalities become apparent. These interventions have the greatest chance of success, they maintain, when policy makers and interventionists use scientific rationality as the primary lever for this work. Therefore, governments should fund basic and applied research toward these ends. Although part of government responsibilities is to provide a social and economic safety net to help individuals and families negotiate changes in economic and social conditions, governments are primarily responsible to prepare individuals to anticipate these changing conditions. The ability to read is fundamental to that preparation, enabling each an equal opportunity to participate in economic and civic life productively under most conditions and to avoid such troubles whenever possible. The rational path to achieve that goal is through scientifically based reading instruction.

> America will become a nation of readers when verified practices of the best teachers in the best schools can be introduced throughout the country. (Anderson et al., 1985)

4

CHARACTER

Conservatives

In this time of moral and political crises, it is the responsibility of the youth of America to affirm certain eternal truths.

We, as young conservatives believe:

That foremost among the transcendent values is the individual's use of his God-given free will, whence derives his right to be free from the restrictions of arbitrary force;

That liberty is indivisible and that political freedom cannot long exist without economic freedom;

That the purpose of government is to protect those freedoms through the preservation of internal order, the provision of national defense, and the administration of justice;

That when government ventures beyond these rightful functions, it accumulates power, which tends to diminish order and liberty;

That the Constitution of the United States is the best arrangement yet devised for empowering government to fulfill its proper role, while restraining it from the concentration and abuse of power;

That the genius of the Constitution—the division of powers—is summed up in the clause that reserves primacy to the several states, or to the people, in those spheres not specifically delegated to the Federal government;

That the market economy, allocating resources by the free play of supply and demand, is the single economic system compatible with the requirements of personal freedom and constitutional government, and that it is at the same time the most productive supplier of human needs;

That when government interferes with the work of the market economy, it tends to reduce the moral and physical strength of the nation; that when it

takes from one man to bestow on another, it diminishes the incentive of the first, the integrity of the second, and the moral authority of both.
(from *The Sharon Statement*, written by M. Stanton Evans and adopted September 11, 1960, at the home of William F. Buckley Jr. in Sharon, CT)

The Sharon Statement (Evans, 1960) catalogs American conservative values: faith in the Christian God, individual liberty, preservation of order through moral authority, national defense and the rule of law, limited government intervention in or regulation of individual liberties, states' rights, and a free market economy. The crisis, William F. Buckley (1955) explained in the initial issue of the *National Review*, was "in essence, the conflict between the Social Engineers, who seek to adjust mankind to conform with scientific utopias, and the disciples of Truth, who defend the organic moral order" (p. 1). People should be free to choose what they value most and accept responsibility for their choices. Because of the diversity among individuals and their free choices, any attempt to develop standard, planned interventions to ameliorate the consequences of those choices among citizens meets the needs of only a few, teaches irresponsibility to all, and wastes social resources. In *The Road to Serfdom with Intellectuals and Socialism* Friedrich Hayek (1944/2007) explained:

> Economic changes, in other words, usually affect only the fringe, the "margin," of our needs. There are many things which are more important than anything, which economic gains or losses are likely to affect, which for us stand high above the amenities and even above the necessities of life which are affected by the economic ups and downs. (p. 94)

Conservatives' representation of poverty is assembled from these originating statements of the modern conservative movement. The poor lack economic resources for two basic reasons. First, for diverse individual reasons, they have chosen not to develop virtues of hard work, individual responsibility, and restraint that enable the free market to supply for their economic needs. Their consequent status in the economy fulfills their valued ends sufficiently. Second, governments' attempts to intervene on the behalf of the poor have undermined their individual integrity and moral authority to choose for themselves, substituting planned choices for their own, and thus, weakened the nation, economically and spiritually. Both reasons combine to create intergenerational, persistent cultures of poverty (Payne, 2005).

These conservative frames for poverty—refusal to accept responsibility for individual choices to prioritize noneconomic needs, and misguided liberal attempts to adjust individuals and society based on scientific prediction—become the targets of conservative action. The poor, then, should receive limited charity in order to provide them with the physical and mental strength to acquire those Protestant values and the opportunity to develop the psychological and social control to let those values bring order to their personal lives. Like all citizens, the poor deserve to be free in order to live according to their personal choices. They should not be subjected to government programs predicted to ameliorate the physical hardship of those choices because those acts limit their liberty and waste community, state, and national resources on failed interventions. Conservatives quote President Reagan: "We waged War on Poverty, and poverty won" (as quoted in Lemann, 1988). On the day of President Obama's second inaugural address, *Weekly Standard* editor William Kristol (2013) explained: "The challenge for American conservatism today is to fulfill both the conservative function of acting as a moral force in an era of dissolution and the reformist function of charting a path up from liberal dissolution" (p. 1).

Between Buckley's opening salvo in 1955 and Kristol's call to action in 2013, wealthy conservatives worked to establish a network with members who would forcefully present the case for conservative principles to the public. This action was intended to counter the work of the "dominant socialist-statist-collectivist orthodoxy" that controlled the media, universities, and public schools. In a *Time for Truth* William Simon (1978) wrote: "Foundations imbued with the philosophy of freedom must take pains to funnel desperately needed fund to scholars, social scientists, writers, and journalists who understand the relationship between political and economic liberty" (p. 230). Since then, conservative businessmen and philanthropic organizations have funded an infrastructure of media corporations and think tanks and endowed academic chairs at universities, law firms, and advocacy groups to define, distribute, and popularize conservative interpretations of every social, economic, and political event and idea. The success of their efforts can be measured in the dominance of conservative representations and frames in continuous public debate over moral issues, scientific findings, and government programs (Alterman, 2002; Lakoff, 2006).

In this chapter I present two parts of a conservative approach to reading and poverty, connect the approach to conservative values, and review the struggle over school curriculum and educational policies since the 1980s. Although there are various subgroups among conservatives, Simon's network of conservative ideas has been effective in developing coalitions among them to project united positions on social, economic, and political issues. Conservative reading education should develop moral character, encourage principled habits and decision making and, then, cultivate the minds of the academically able, who will build slowly and carefully on the triumphs of the Western past. The federal and state governments' role is only to ensure that the school curriculum is rigorous and that each student is evaluated fairly based on his or her intellectual capacity and ability to profit from further instruction. These conservative policy priorities are embedded in the Reagan Administration's shift of Title 1 from targeted programs to block grants and the recommendations of The National Commission on Excellence in Education's (NCEE) *A Nation at Risk* report.

Conservative Reading Education

The Family

> This is rude to say, but here's what this is all about: Millions of parents don't have the means, the skill or, in some cases, the interest in building their children's future. Early childhood education is about building structures so both parents and children learn practical life skills. It's about getting kids from disorganized homes into rooms with kids from organized homes so good habits will rub off. It's about instilling achievement values where they are absent. (Brooks, 2013, A17)

Brooks's statement implies that parents are responsible for organizing their households to support their children's future. That responsibility requires income to provide adequate food, shelter, and health care, enabling each child to develop physically and cognitively. According to conservatives, the source of that income is important because it provides implicit lessons for children about how society functions. If the income is earned and needs are provided through the structures of work, planning, and restraint, then homes are organized by these virtues, which "rub off" on children through daily example. Regardless of income level, these achievements are worthy of celebration at home and in communities because they are the basic building blocks that enable society to function. Responsible parents make responsible children who acquire practical skills, enabling them to take advantage of social institutions designed to help them prosper throughout life. Part of the American Dream is that parents prepare their children to achieve more than previous generations.

Parents are to bring order to their children's lives, helping them to manage time and space in ways that are practical and considerate of others. This takes patience, consistency, and skill. Regardless of which psychological theory parents employ, infants, toddlers, and children take time to adapt to the order of their environments, connecting responses to stimuli correctly through consistent reinforcement or approximating theories of how life works through explicit and implicit feedback. Children learn routines of behaviors and actions, modes of thought, and facility with language appropriate for the company they keep, the time of day, and the places they explore, developing expectations about how they can fit in appropriately. Eventually, children learn to attend independently to clues that enable them to function throughout their days. Children cannot raise themselves and be functional. Raising children happens best when parents engage their children in physical and verbal interaction skillfully. Through routines, play, and talk with their parents, children learn how to act, think, and narrate their lives appropriately and productively.

Beyond means and skills, parents must take an active interest in raising their children properly—an interest that sets family priorities. Parents must model the virtues, thoughts, and actions they intend to instill in their children, making each obvious to their children through deed as well as word. Regardless of personal interest, parents must commit to marriage, work, and discipline in their own lives so that their children can reap the benefits in their development. This does not mean that parents should indulge all of their children's desires, placing them above their own. Rather, families are most effective when children serve as apprentices to their parents' mastery of examples of good living. Within the order of such households, conservatives argue, there is little need for preschool education.

Yet, in his *New York Times* op-ed essay, Brooks echoes Kristof's conclusion after his trip to Kentucky, reporting that millions of American parents cannot, do not, or will not raise their children in ways that prepare them to take advantage of schooling and other social institutions. Beyond personal tragedy, parental neglect brings immediate and future social and economic problems for communities and states. Therefore, under certain conditions, Brooks welcomes federal government support for state models of preschool education. "The essential thing is to build systems that can measure progress, learn and adapt to local circumstances" (Brooks, 2013, A17). He warns against continued or increased funding for the federal model, Head Start, because recent government evaluations (Head Start, 2012) demonstrated that it produced only modest increases in low-income children's readiness for school, and those modest advantages disappeared by the third grade. American Enterprise Institute pundit Charles Murray (2013) concedes that increased Head Start funding might buy "a few hours a day in a safer, warmer, and more nurturing environment," but after 50 years of that program, Americans still don't know how to substitute for traditional familial methods of raising children. Rather, he concludes, "we have to think about how we increase the odds that children are born to present, caring, and competent parents" (Murray, 2013).

Over the past 30 years, Murray has summarized the conservative answers to that question. The liberal policies of the 1960s Great Society and War on Poverty have undermined the integrity of individuals and the social foundation of marriage, rendering more and more Americans unable to perform their traditional responsibilities in their homes, communities, and society. In *Losing Ground,* Murray (1984) explained how social scientists "discovered" that poverty was a structural problem rather than an individual responsibility, shifting the solutions for poverty from individual rehabilitation to a transfer of income and wealth from those advantaged by the system—working, middle, and upper-class families—to those suffering from discrimination in their access to the economy. The subsequent liberal policies invited a moral decline among the poor that deepened their personal poverty and extended it across generations. To increase the odds that children have competent parents, Murray concluded, the policies of welfare—income, food, shelter, and health care—should be curtailed and eventually eliminated. These acts would provide space and incentives for the poor to regain their traditional values.

In *The Bell Curve* Herrnstein and Murray (1995) argued that liberals' attempts to provide equal opportunity for all to participate within the institutions designed to foster success became policies to ensure equal outcomes among unequal participants. Targeted programs, affirmative action, and social promotion policies papered over the realities of inequalities in the genetic and moral endowments among individuals, artificially creating unrealistic expectations among Americans concerning their intellectual abilities and economic possibilities and, therefore, wasting resources on those who could not possibly profit from the opportunities afforded them or fulfill the responsibilities thrust on them. Herrnstein and Murray (1995) concluded:

> It is time for America once again to try living with inequality, as life is lived; understanding that each human being has strengths and weaknesses, qualities we admire and qualities we do not admire, competencies and incompetencies, assets and debits; that success of each human life is not measured externally but internally; that of all the rewards we can confer on each other, the most precious is a place as a valued fellow citizen. (pp. 551–552)

In order to encourage responsible parents, equal outcome policies should be eliminated and society should honor traditional civic contributions among people of all economic classes.

Coming Apart provides Murray (2012) with a new metaphor to describe the logical, but unfortunate, outcome of 50 years of injurious liberal social policy. The "crisis" of the 1960s has become the dissolution of American society in 2012, the coming apart of America because the poorest 30 percent of the American public have lost touch with the four "founding virtues"—marriage, industriousness, honesty, and religious conviction—while the richest 20 percent have recommitted to those values that enabled American exceptionalism. Because people seek to associate with others like themselves, Murray reiterates from *The Bell Curve* that income segregation brings cultural segregation in which the virtues of the rich are not visible to the poor, who have few community examples of how they might overcome the consequences of rising rates of divorce, unemployment, lawlessness, and spiritual emptiness. Without those models for recovery, American society splits culturally and cannot repair itself. Murray chides Brooks, Kristof, and the well-to-do to be proud of the virtues, to stop thinking "it's rude" to name this problem, and to start demonstrating the solution publicly.

Books of Virtue

Former Secretary of Education William Bennett offers stories and literacy to fill this void. He reaches back to Aristotle to explain his plan. Aristotle argued that good moral character is developed through habits of mind. To develop a moral society, education should develop intelligent patterns of moral choice guided by attachment and love. These patterns are learned through moral apprenticeships within families and civilized communities that display and reward good moral choices. To carry good moral principles beyond the boundaries of family and community, great moral tales are composed, shared, and memorized, leading all toward good moral habits of thought and behavior. Acting on this model, Bennett (1994) collected tales from "the corpus of Western Civilization, that American schoolchildren once upon a time, knew by heart" (p. 15). To ensure a moral society, parents, ministers, club leaders, and teachers would read these stories aloud or together and present their moral principles explicitly to children and youth.

Bennett's (1994) first anthology, *The Book of Virtues,* contains stories, essays, and poems selected for their "moral moorings and anchors that have never been more necessary" (p. 12). *The Moral Compass,* his second, presents stories "aimed at clear concepts of good and bad without hesitation or apology. They treat life as a moral endeavor" (Bennett, 1995a, p. 12). The third volume, a picture book titled *The Children's Book of Virtues,* includes a few of the stories from the original that "speak to morality and virtue not as something to have but as something to be, the most important thing to be" (Bennett, 1995b, p. 6). Together, Bennett (1994) designed these texts to "continue the task of preserving the principles, the ideals, and notions of goodness and greatness we hold dear" (p. 12).

Bennett does not equivocate in naming these virtues: self-discipline, compassion, responsibility, friendship, work, courage, perseverance, honesty, loyalty, and faith. To help the reader recognize the virtue embedded in each selection, Bennett organized the classics into sections under the headings of a single virtue—with tens of examples for each category. To aid readers' and listeners' interpretations, Bennett provides a two-paged introduction to the virtue and then a short specific blurb before each entry. Each category offers a broad assortment of authors: George Washington on civility, Martin Luther King Jr. on perseverance, Dolley Madison and Susan B. Anthony on courage, Abraham Lincoln on compassion, Oscar Wilde on friendship, and Chuck Colson and Mary Wollstonecraft on faith. He instructs buyers on how to read the book properly. "This volume is not intended to be a book one reads from cover to cover. It is, rather, a book for browsing, for marking favorite passages, for reading aloud to family, for memorizing pieces here and there" (Bennett, 1994, p. 15).

On page 177 under the heading "Compassion," Bennett presents and interprets a letter from Abraham Lincoln to Mrs. Bixby, consoling her on the loss of five sons who fought for the Union Army during the American Civil War. In his introduction to the letter, Bennett quotes Carl Sandburg, "the letter wore its awful implication that human freedom so often was paid for with agony," to direct readers' orientation toward the text. Lincoln wrote:

> I feel how weak and fruitless must be any word of mine which should attempt to beguile you from grief of a loss so overwhelming. But I cannot refrain from tendering you the consolations that may be found in the thanks

of the republic they died to save. I . . . leave you . . . the solemn pride that must be yours to have laid so costly a sacrifice upon the altar of freedom. (Bennett, 1994, p. 177)

Bennett acknowledges that Lincoln had been misinformed about the Bixby sons (two were killed, one was imprisoned, and two deserted); yet, he assumes that families could discuss Lincoln's personal condolences to Mrs. Bixby, a father's empathy for a mother (Lincoln's son was about to enlist), and a president's sympathy to all families during war. Beyond the virtues, Bennett sees benefit in families sitting together, listening to the stories and each other, and talking about words and ideas of celebrated and sophisticated texts of the past.

Many Americans bought and browsed *The Book of Virtues,* which spent 88 consecutive weeks on the *New York Times* bestseller list (tied for 30th place for longest run on that chart). Despite this success, the moral lessons required readers with sophisticated reading abilities and discussion leadership to make the virtues available to children. In order to vary the stimulus and to overcome problems of access to the sophisticated rhetorical styles and complexities of some of the texts selected, Porchlight Entertainment (with funding from the conservative Olin Foundation) produced *Adventures from the Book of Virtues,* an animated television series for PBS. Each show explored a virtue within the context of two elementary school–aged children's everyday lives. When confronted with a moral dilemma, the children turned to one or more of four anthropomorphic mountain animals, which would present a relevant lesson in the form of a story or poem (paraphrased from *The Book of Virtues*). Through this format, reading skills were bypassed because the virtues were named, the relevance identified clearly, and the applications to daily life were made explicit. The series ran for three seasons (1996–2000 with production gaps) and is now available on the Internet for all to use.

The texts and episodes are expected to show what virtues look like, what they are in practice, how to recognize them, and how they work. Although adults and children are encouraged to talk about each virtue during and after reading or viewing, they should not debate them. Rather, each text or episode makes the rewards for living virtuously readily apparent, and the punishments for poor choices equally clear. Bennett (1994) calls these virtues "the basics."

> The reader scanning this book may notice that it does not discuss issues like nuclear war, abortion, creationism or euthanasia. . . . But the fact is that the formation of character in young people is educationally a different task from, and a prior task to, the discussion of, the great, difficult ethical controversies of the day. First things first. And planting the ideas of virtue, of good traits in the young, comes first. . . . This is a book of basics. The tough issues can, if teachers and parents wish, be taken up later. And I would add, a person who is morally literate will be immeasurably better equipped than a

morally illiterate person to reach a reasoned and ethically defensible position on these tough issues. (pp. 12–13)

Coming to School

The role of early schooling is to determine who among the students have benefited from discussing and practicing traditional virtues and who have not. Those deemed to have started are considered school ready, possessing academic advantages in disposition, language, and values over their uninitiated peers (Payne, 2005). Teachers start the advantaged immediately on a path to becoming an educated person by teaching them to crack the codes of literature, mathematics, society, and nature. That path builds on the solid foundation brought from home, laying out yearly, monthly, and weekly goals to meet across the grades. Each student will progress as far as his or her drive and endowments will take them through the curriculum. As Murray explained, local traditions and conditions will determine the eventual economic fate of these graduates, but through this curriculum, all will achieve civic validation.

However, if students are judged to have missed the benefits of an ordered family life (Brooks, 2013), then teachers attempt to compensate for poor parenting in order to help them catch up with their peers. Teachers begin the missing regime of virtues by reading aloud from *The Book of Virtues* and its equivalent, by having clear rules for expected classroom behaviors, and by engaging in daily conversations about both. In Brooks's words, teachers bring order to their lives, working on their dispositions, language, and values. Neuman and Celano (2012) named this "paternalistic schooling," connoting that the school officials and teachers become default parents in order to prepare these students to succeed at school and later in life. According to their academic interests and intellectual abilities, some or many disadvantaged students could eventually become educated as well, but all will benefit immediately from these moral lessons. To neglect this duty, conservatives argue (Payne, 2005), condemns these individuals to academic and economic failure with, as Murray explained, profound social consequences.

In addition to providing this moral support, teachers must overcome the limits of parents' language use. Based on studies of talk in homes (e.g., Hart & Risley, 1995), teachers must support disadvantaged students on four linguistic levels before they can begin to participate effectively in the regular curriculum track. These children have not heard enough talk, the talk they have heard is limited in its grammatical complexity as well as its lexical variety, and the statements have been restricted in their linguistic function. As a consequence, students have not acquired school-ready language. Teachers must teach them language directly, providing lessons on how to pronounce the phonemes in words properly, to master standard grammatical structures, to expand their vocabularies (estimated to be only one-third of that of their advantaged peers when they start school), and to develop rhetorical forms appropriate for various school situations. Without these lessons, disadvantaged students cannot make the transition from the oral traditions of home to written traditions of school, and unless the instruction begins immediately when they enter school and is fast paced, they will continue to fall farther behind their peers on the expected curriculum.

Regardless of the content of these lessons, teachers must incorporate the dispositions, language, and values they hope to teach with the design of each lesson. The format of the lesson must require and support students' efforts to become self-disciplined in body and mind, insisting that they sit attentively, engage appropriately, and prepare for their turns. Teachers must make clear that each student is responsible for his or her actions and learning, but show compassion for students who struggle in their responses or mastery. Challenging lesson content encourages students to develop resilience and persistence to overcome barriers. Always, teachers must be honest with their appraisal of students' progress, demonstrating how students can develop independence and pride in their efforts and accomplishments. During lessons, teachers' language must be varied in grammatical form and word choice and precise in description and requests, demonstrating appropriate ways in which students should communicate at school. Finally, lessons should be designed around a single clear goal and carefully sequenced from beginning to end. By creating well-designed lessons, teachers instill order into the lives of disadvantaged children.

These remedial steps enable the disadvantaged to eventually proceed to the basics. As Bennett argued, students should not be asked to consider sophisticated topics or innovative ways of learning until they have mastery of the basics. In conservative reading education, this means that students have proper dispositions—they can show up on time ready to learn, sit attentively for regular periods of time, defer gratification until they have mastered a task, and persevere after constructive feedback. They have a reasonable grasp of standard oral English appropriate for their age, pronouncing words correctly, speaking in complete sentences, demonstrating appropriate and varied word choice, and shifting their language appropriately to match the situation. They have started productively to crack the codes when reading and writing simple written texts at word, sentence, paragraph, and passage levels. They take pride in their deportment and their accomplishments. To advance beyond the remedial track, they have accepted the order that others brought from home and are prepared to become educated.

Becoming an Educated Person

> Children start off in the position of barbarians outside the gates. The problem is to get them inside the citadel of civilization so that they will understand and love what they see when they get there. (Peters, 1965, p. 107)

Through her many books on education, Diane Ravitch has performed Kristol's charges for today's conservatives. For three decades, she has been a moral force for the best traditions of public education in times of relativism (*The Schools We Deserve,* 1987; *The American Reader,* 1990/2000; 2000; *The English Reader,* 2006) as well as a critic of radical (*The Revisionists Revised,* 1978), liberal (*Left Back,* 2000), and neoliberal (*The Death and Life of the Great American School System,* 2010) efforts to reform public schools based on equality, science, and the market. While she articulates and advocates for conservative traditions of teaching the basics, Ravitch concentrates primarily on the potential of the traditional liberal arts to educate the barbarians after they have accepted the order in the citadel. Like Murray and Peters, Ravitch acknowledges that because of differences in intelligence and will, not all barbarians will accept that order, and not all who accept that order will realize the full potential of schooling. However, all should, she believes, have access to the best schooling has to offer and will benefit from that association as long as they are willing and able.

Ravitch recommends a rigorous curriculum in which students learn the ideas, values, and practices of cultural and academic disciplines in order to make sense of, appreciate, and adapt their lives. Plato wrote about this model in *The Republic,* discussing the captive in the cave seeking knowledge that would lead him from darkness to the light. This is an apt metaphor for conservative hopes for schooling—to lead students out of the darkness of incivility and ignorance into the light of cultural traditions and knowledge that make society possible. With a sufficient number of enlightened free individuals, conservatives argue, citizens can overcome barbarism and avoid scientism. Conservative schooling provides the educated with the moral and social security to prevent "the war of all against all" individualism and, simultaneously, instill in them a love of personal freedom against the standardization of social life. To fulfill this potential, public schools must provide access to and supports for a varied and balanced curriculum that includes study of the arts, humanities, mathematics, natural sciences, and social sciences in each grade. Because all the disciplines are necessary, school officials and teachers must keep each discipline equally attractive, connecting each to personal and social development.

To be considered educated, then, students must take up the ideas and practices within each discipline, coming to understand its history, its ethics, and its relationships with other disciplines as well as its practices. The curriculum must require students to read deeply and discuss the classic texts of each discipline, to follow their trajectory into the current interpretations and innovations, and to imagine how they might be useful to address contemporary aesthetic, social, and natural problems.

> The only serious solution is the one that is almost universally rejected: the good old Great Books approach, in which a liberal education means reading certain generally recognized classic texts, just reading them, letting them

dictate what questions are and the method of approaching them—not forcing them into categories we make up, not treating them as historical products, but trying to read them as their authors wished them to be read. (Bloom, 1987, p. 344)

The Great Books Foundation is a nonprofit organization incorporated in 1947 to develop civil discourse among citizens through shared inquiry while reading important texts. The organization published inexpensive paperback copies of classic Western literature and developed discussion procedures based on the Socratic method in order to help adults from "all walks of life" engage with the best ideas of the past. Robert Mayer Hutchins and Mortimer Adler designed the reading list from the University of Chicago's liberal arts curriculum, encouraging participants to listen to others' opinions on the meaning of the selections, consider as many points of view as possible, weigh the available evidence within the text for interpretations, and modify their understandings accordingly. Without imparting information or presenting their opinions, trained discussion leaders could help adults to find common ground through systematic and sustained engagement with the virtues that make civil society possible. The Foundation has since broadened its reading list from the original to include women authors, texts from non-Western cultures, and contemporary as well as classic texts, and now provides published guides to help leaders work with these new texts.

In 1962 the Foundation produced Junior Great Books text sets for students in Grades 5–9. Originally, the Junior curriculum was selected from shorter works of the Great Books authors with shared inquiry adapted to the developmental age of the participants. Since the 1980s, the Foundation has expanded the curriculum in two ways. Its reading list has become more inclusive and the programs are now spread across all elementary and secondary school grades (K–1 read-aloud program, 2 transition, 3–5 consolidation, 6–8 roundtable discussions, and 9–12 introduction to the adult program). In order to accommodate the shared inquiry during the elementary years, the teacher guides include more basic reading instruction to prepare for discussions (prereading, note taking, fluency tips, vocabulary development, scaffolding with written assignments, discussion, and process debriefing). The goals remain the same throughout—to promote civil discourse in order to build participants' capacities to imagine and live good lives.

This is decidedly intellectual work—the development of one's mind—and it is what makes students more civilized, even more human, than those who specialize in one area too soon or who favor the practical and vocational. The educated become distinguished from others not so much by what they do as by what they see and grasp in the world and by how understandings of beauty, meaning, logic, nature, and human interactions inform that gaze. With all this in mind, the educated can then become creative, posing novel interpretations of the past, present, and future.

> The pupil must gradually get the grammar of the activity into his guts so that he can eventually win through to the stage of autonomy, but he cannot do this unless he has mastered the moves made by his predecessors, which are enshrined in the living traditions. (Peters, 1965, p. 109)

Because no less than civilization is at stake, conservatives revere good public school teachers in their communities. Good teachers live moral, educated lives within the public view, serving as examples to all community members. They are responsible to the living traditions, translating structures and codes in their classrooms, while they inspire devotion among their students to their social and civic powers. Conservatives find it hard to quantify these qualities of good teachers because they do not advocate a single formula for teaching all subjects. Rather, conservatives know the good teachers from experience. Ravitch (2010) writes about her favorite English teacher who taught with love for her subject and tough love for her students. "Mrs. Ratliff did nothing for our self-esteem. She challenged us to meet her exacting standards. I think she imagined herself bringing enlightenment to barbarians (that was us)" (p. 169). Rather than lecture and test, Mrs. Ratliff introduced her students to Shakespeare, Keats, Shelley, Wordsworth, and Milton, mediated their reading, led their discussions, and required them to write essays of criticism. Her responses to student essays were demanding yet supportive, conveying to each student that she believed he or she could, with more effort, develop an understanding of literature and a command of criticism. Because of her expertise and technique, capable students flocked to her classes. For each graduating senior, Mrs. Ratliff copied a line of poetry as a gift. Ravitch received "To strive, to seek, to find, and not to yield" (Tennyson's "Ulysses") and "among them, but not of them" (Byron's "Childe Harold's Pilgrimage").

> As she did in class, Mrs. Ratliff used the moment to show us how literature connected to our own lives, without condescending into shallow "relevance." I think these [poetry lines] were the best graduation presents I got, because they are the only ones I remember a half-century later. (Ravitch, 2010, p. 170)

In effect, Mrs. Ratliff's graduation gift names standards for conservative teachers. They are "to strive, to seek, to find, and not to yield" in order to, in Buckley's words, "defend the organic moral order." As Murray suggested, this means accepting responsibility to bring order to life among the poor, and not apologizing for insisting on educational programs that build character from traditional American values. This echoes Kristol's reformist challenge for conservatives; good teachers should be "among them, but not of them," molding low-income children's dispositions, extending their language toward standard English, and, thus, preparing them for the traditional school curriculum afforded their advantaged peers. For those students who accept this order, teachers can then begin the basics, leading, for those capable, to an educated life. Endowed with intelligence and a grasp of structure and codes of academic disciplines, educated conservatives can begin "charting a path up from liberal dissolution." To neglect conservative reading education is to invite social, political, and economic ruin.

Conservative Reading Education Policy

The reports from the Committee of Ten (1893) and the Committee of Fifteen (1895) are the touchstones of conservative reading education policy. Representing the National Education Association, these committees attempted to set curricular standards for secondary and elementary schools that would produce an educated populous in a rapidly changing America. The reports are noteworthy for their commitment to conservative values—the systematic development of reasoning power, sensitivity to beauty, and high moral character—while reaching out to previously neglected groups. Beyond the basic skills that enabled children to cipher and read and write standard English, all students were to study mathematics, geography, history, grammar, sciences, languages, literature, and the arts. Although less than half of elementary school graduates would progress to secondary school, and less than a quarter of secondary school graduates would enroll in college, the entire public school curriculum pointed toward college readiness because those were the skills and the knowledge that made society possible. "Every subject which is taught at all in a secondary school should be taught in the same way and to the same extent to every pupil so long as he pursues it, no matter what the probable destination of the pupil may be, or at what point his education is to cease" (Committee of Ten, 1893, p. 17).

In *Left Back,* Ravitch (2000) describes the century-long, progressive assault on the Committees' recommendations that she blames for the contemporary crisis in public education. Advocates for a child-centered approach to education, she reports, inverted conservative assumptions about human nature. Rather than performing a civilizing service by initiating barbarians into the benefits of society as conservatives believed, child-centered advocates charged that traditional school curriculum corrupted the innocence of children by exposing them too soon to the "barbarism" of society—competition, violence, and materialism. According to child-centered educators, the conservative teachers have it backwards, forcing students to know the foibles of society before they learn to know and love themselves and, thus, making them susceptible to social temptation. A child-centered curriculum should follow Rousseau's (1762/1979) advice in *Emile,* "You have not got to teach him truths so much as to show him how to set about discovering them for himself" (p. 131). For child-centered advocates, individual creativity should precede rather than follow the study of traditions.

Advocates for scientific management in education challenged the process and product of the conservative curriculum. Rather than setting curriculum according to a consensus among committees of experts, educators should employ science to determine objectively: What is taught? How is it taught? By whom? To whom? And toward what end? In this way, schools become more efficient and more effective in meeting individuals' and society's needs. Employing this logic, advocates challenged the contents of the traditional curriculum, the traditional organization of schooling, and the Committees' assumptions that all students could benefit from the same curriculum regardless of their talents and interests. Educators should let the data decide.

> The judgments of science are distinguished from other judgments by being more impartial, more objective, more precise, and more subject to verification by any competent observer and being made by those who by their nature and training should be better judges. Science knows or should know no favorites and cares for nothing in its conclusions but the truth. (Thorndike, 1906, p. 265)

Radicals charged that the conservative curriculum reproduced the existing social inequities among groups by feeding the ideologies of the past to each new generation as if they were fact, nature, and truth. Rather than enlightenment, the contents of the conservative curriculum were sets of ideas and values that served to justify and support the social, economic, and political status quo. Radicals worried that the longer marginalized groups remained within the conservative curriculum, the more likely it became that they would accept their lack of opportunity and benefit as personal failures rather than the result of structural problems. Therefore, a radical curriculum—one designed to help all students—should engage students in consideration of structural issues of inequality and seek the redistribution of social and economic benefits more justly. "Neutrality with respect to the great issues which agitate society is practically tantamount to giving support to the most powerful forces engaged in the contest" (Counts, 1932, p. 263).

Ravitch (2000) traces these progressive critiques across the 20th century, demonstrating how child-centered approaches led to moral relativism and the relevance curriculum, scientific management turned school curriculum and teaching into the mechanical assembly of skills without knowledge, and radical concerns brought identity politics and political correctness at the expense of Western values and traditions. As each of these foolhardy critiques became embedded in state and federal education policies (Ravitch, 2007), conservative reading education became less likely in American public schools. Ravitch points with horror at the current state of public schooling—the absence of required reading lists at each grade level (Ravitch, 1990/2000), multiple choice testing as evidence of learning (Ravitch, 2010), and textbook review processes that remove any content that seems possibly objectionable to any interest group (Ravitch, 2004).

As states and local communities resisted these liberal policies, progressives pressed courts to intervene, arguing for expanded federal roles into public schools in order to ensure that all students could reap the predicted benefits. Because education is a state's right, federal authorities offered increased funding to states and school districts in exchange for compliance. These financial incentives, which started as supplemental, quickly became hard lines in state and district education budgets, making it difficult for states and schools to choose their own educational directions. Over time, Ravitch argues, public schools became more progressive, more standardized, and less intellectual, and as a direct result the knowledge gap widened between public and private school curricula, ensuring that students from financially able families would be much more likely to become educated than their low-income peers. To save public schools and American exceptionalism, then, Ravitch and other conservatives work to overturn liberal and radical policies and to restore a contemporary version of recommendations from the Committees of Ten and Fifteen.

Reagan and the 1980s

> First the President wanted to reduce substantially federal spending for education. Second, he wanted to strengthen local and state control of education and to reduce dramatically the federal responsibility in this area. Third, the President wanted to maintain a limited federal role that would build and enhance the capacity of states to carry out their traditional responsibilities. Fourth, the President wanted to encourage the establishment of laws and rules that would offer greatly expanded parental choice and that would increase competition for students among schools in newly created public and private structures patterned after the free market system that motivates and disciplines U.S. business and industry. Fifth, President Reagan wanted to encourage a substantial reduction in federal judicial activity in education. Finally, the President wanted to abolish the U.S. Department of Education and replace it with a newly established agency that would be less powerful and prominent in the total structure of the federal government. (Bell, 1986, p. 488)

President Reagan's goals can be read as a conservative campaign to reverse the progressive agenda in schools and to rewrite federal liberal policies in order to increase students' access to conservative reading education. Many of these priorities originated in the conservative network of philanthropic foundations (e.g., Abell, Coors, and Olin), think tanks (American Enterprise Institute, Cato Institute, and Heritage Foundation), and religious foundations (700 Club, Billy Graham Crusade, and Moral Majority). In documents submitted to President Reagan's transition team, the Cato Institute proposed vouchers for poor families to replace Head Start programs, and the Heritage Foundation called for stipends for the poor in order to replace Title 1 programs with private tutors. When William Bennett became Reagan's second Secretary of Education, he celebrated "a grassroots movement for education reform that has generated a renewed commitment to excellence, character, and fundamentals" (Bennett, 1988, p. 9).

The Reagan Administration used the reauthorization of the Elementary and Secondary Education Act (ESEA) (called the Educational Consolidation and Improvement Act [ECIA] of 1981) to pursue these goals. The new Act reduced federal authority and cut 15 percent from federal education spending. Chapter 1 replaced Title 1 and reversed the original assumptions that federal oversight was necessary in order to improve low-income students' reading achievement. Rather, Chapter 1 assumed that the first 15 years of ESEA had built state and local capacity sufficiently that they could design fair and effective compensatory instructional programs to fit local needs. To enable state and local choices, Chapter 2 of the ECIA collapsed 29 targeted programs that had been funded separately into single block grants to states. The formula for funding remained the same—states received Chapter 2 allotments according to the number of low-income students enrolled in its schools. However, state officials were not regulated on how they dispensed the federal funds among schools.

Chapters 1 and 2 purposely altered the dynamic of concern for helping low-income struggling readers, moving the focus from tutoring individuals and small groups to school-wide initiatives. This move was necessary, the Reagan Administration argued, because the original Title 1 had created an entrenched federal bureaucracy in public schools with little incentive to solve the problem for which the ESEA was originally designed. Under Title 1, schools received federal funding based solely on the number of struggling low-income students enrolled. Each success, then, diminished the need for the program and its employees, and the identification of every new struggling reader increased those needs. Similar to conservative criticisms of all federal intervention programs, the ESEA actually hurt the ones it was intended to help. Chapter 1 reversed that logic, connecting funding to students' reading achievement across the entire school. Funding would follow successes rather than reward continued failures. By focusing on conservative views of school readiness and its demand of the basics for all in public elementary schools, Chapter 1 and Chapter 2 would gradually overcome the problems that the original ESEA had created, freeing states and local schools to concentrate on fixing the problems of progressive policies wrought on high school curriculum and pedagogy.

A Nation at Risk

> All, regardless of race or class or economic status, are entitled to a fair chance and to the tools for developing their individual powers of mind and spirit to the utmost. This promise means that all children by virtue of their own efforts, competently guided, can hope to attain the mature and informed judgment needed to secure gainful employment, and to manage their own lives, thereby serving not only their own interests but also the progress of society itself. (The National Commission on Excellence in Education, 1983)

The Reagan Administration's plan to devolve decision-making authority to the state and local level through Chapters 1 and 2 did not prevent officials from criticizing the state of public high schools. A year after ECIA was implemented, Secretary of Education Terrell Bell released the NCEE's *A Nation at Risk* report, which concluded "the educational foundations of our society are presently being eroded by a rising tide of mediocrity that threatens our very future as a Nation and a people" (The National Commission on Excellence in Education, 1983, p. 1). The indicators of decline were many:

- American students were never ranked first on international tests, but were ranked last seven times.
- Twenty-three million American adults were illiterate.
- Average scores on standardized tests were lower than the generation before.
- Only 60 percent of 17-year-olds could draw inferences from written material; 20 percent could write a cogent persuasive essay; and 33 percent could solve a multiple-step mathematical problem.
- Colleges and the military wasted millions of dollars on remedial classes and training for underprepared high school graduates.

The NCEE warned that this decline would have personal consequences—"individuals in our society who do not possess the levels of skill, literacy, and training essential to this new era will be effectively disenfranchised, not simply from the material rewards that accompany competent performance, but also from the chance to participate fully in our national life." There would be equally important national economic consequences as well—"our once unchallenged preeminence in commerce, industry, science and technological innovation is being overtaken." Beyond the economic, "[our concern] includes the intellectual, moral and spiritual strengths of our people which knit together the very fabric of society." "All who care about America and its future" should demand change.

The NCEE blamed the liberalization of content, expectations, time, and teaching since the 1960s as the primary cause of the problems. The Commission found that the curriculum had been "homogenized, diluted, and diffused" in order to accommodate more diverse student enrollments. Moreover, the "cafeteria style curriculum" permitted students to choose "appetizers and desserts" for the main courses in their plan of study. Because state graduation requirements became minimal, few students chose a rigorous schedule—few high school students completed more than a year or two of math and social studies and a single year of science. Students filled the remainder of their course schedule with electives—learning how to cook, hammer, type, and drive. In comparison with other industrialized countries, the American public school day was two hours shorter, the school year had at least one less month of school days, and serious homework had disappeared in many classes. Moreover, changing opportunities for women and attempts to diversify the teacher core had significantly diminished the quality of school personnel. Colleges of education did not recruit able students to teacher certification programs; those programs swapped teaching methods classes for academic course work with rigorous intellectual content, and "the professional working life of teachers [was] on the whole unacceptable."

The NCEE's recommendations echoed the scope of the Committee of Ten a century earlier. "We must demand the best effort and performance for all students whether they are gifted or less able, affluent or disadvantaged, whether destined for college, the farm or industry" (The National Commission on Excellence in Education, 1983). States and local districts were challenged to adopt rigorous measurable standards for graduation and for each course in the curriculum. Students should study four years of English; three years of mathematics, science, and social studies; and add a year of computer science and two of foreign language (if they intended to enroll in college). The school day should be lengthened by an hour and the school year increased by 20–40 days. Teachers should assign homework for each class daily. Teachers' colleges should increase both their entrance requirements and the number of academic courses, leaving the pedagogical training for internships with master teachers. Teacher salaries should be raised and contracts extended to 11 months, ensuring adequate time for annual professional development. The only difference between the NCEE's and the Committee of Ten's recommendations was the absence of courses on Latin and grammar.

Although the federal government would be expected to supply technical expertise, to ensure equity among groups and to collect and share data nationally, states and local districts would remain primarily responsible for making these changes. The NCEE cautioned patience and persistence. "Reform of our educational system will take time and unwavering commitment. It will require equally widespread, energetic, and dedicated action." To drive government and local officials to make these changes, the NCEE wrote directly to parents, imploring them to demand changes in order to provide their children with a chance to become educated, and therefore, able to negotiate the increasing complexities of work and social life. Ultimately, however, individual students would be responsible for their choices. "Take hold of your life, apply your gifts and talents, work with dedication and self-discipline."

Conservatives used *A Nation at Risk* in two ways. First, the report's patriotic language and statistics afforded them evidence that public schools were failed federal government monopolies that lacked passion for traditional values and had lowered the achievement of high school graduates. "Our once unchallenged preeminence," "rising tide of mediocrity," and "an act of war" grabbed the attention of the media in ways that previous reports on American public schools had not. While Chapter 1 and Chapter 2 enabled the Reagan Administration to act on its first three educational objectives (cut federal spending, increase state and local control, and build local capacity), *A Nation at Risk* presented empirical evidence, suggesting that the federal pursuit of equity over excellence in schools had backfired and implying a need for families to choose alternatives to failing public schools. President Reagan (1983) used the release of the report to restate these claims without acknowledging that *A Nation at Risk* was silent about "tuition tax credits, vouchers, educational savings accounts, voluntary school prayer, or abolishing the Department of Education."

Second, conservatives used the NCEE's recommendations to design a path out of the liberal dissolution of public schools. Years later, Ravitch (2010) lamented: "Every one of its recommendations was within the scope of the schools as they existed then and as they exist now, and none had the potential to harm public education" (p. 28). Rather than invite federal expertise, the NCEE assumed that states and districts cared about students, were capable of setting rigorous academic standards, and could choose appropriate assessments to determine whether those standards had been met. Therefore, the states and districts, not the federal government, should control school reform. Liberal strategies for academic tracking among groups of students were unnecessary and discriminatory because all students would benefit from the same academic curriculum.

Rather than the liberal hodgepodge curriculum, the NCEE presented clear academic goals in succinct terms, leaving the specifics for school personnel to determine locally. For example, the teaching of English "should equip graduates to (a) comprehend, interpret, evaluate, and use what they read; (b) write well organized, effective papers; (c) listen effectively and discuss ideas intelligently; and (d) know our literary heritage and how it enhances imagination and ethical understanding, and how it relates to the customs, ideas, and values of today's life and culture." With these goals, parents, teachers, and students could all understand what students were expected to know and do.

In order to deliver on these promises, liberal plans to diversify the teaching corps would be replaced by more rigorous entrance and exit requirements to become a teacher. Beginning teachers would demonstrate greater competence in the subject(s) they would teach before they were asked to develop their abilities to present lessons and keep order. Rather than working through liberal unions, teachers' salaries and working conditions would be tied to peer review and local conditions, allowing a natural order of talent to emerge—"so that superior teachers can be rewarded, average ones encouraged, and poor ones either improved or terminated." By working from the NCEE's recommendations, conservatives could return order and purpose to public schools, increasing discipline within individuals, reestablishing American founding virtues in the hearts and minds of each student, and regaining America's economic and social advantages among all nations.

After A Nation at Risk

According to Ravitch (2010), this conservative path toward school reform was detoured before it could reach the conservative reading education needed for an educated America. What began as a voluntary call to duty for state and local officials to remake high schools became a legal mandate of world-class standards, basic skills, high stakes testing, and market regimes among and within schools. Although traces of these elements could be found in the NCEE's report, all were to be harnessed in the common effort to make high school a place to develop intellectual and moral competence in all students. As each detour became more prominent in debates about and actions for school reform during the 1990s, the possibilities of conservative reading education became more remote.

Standards

The NCEE proclaimed America to be a nation at risk of losing its standing in the world because public high school standards had declined dramatically during the previous generation. Without raising standards, graduates would be unable to compete in a global innovation economy or to deliberate thoughtfully within a democracy. Although these threats were national in scope, any legal solution had to be located within each state. This obvious tension was "resolved" in 1991 when the federal Department of Education awarded grants to develop voluntary national standards in seven subjects (the arts, civics, English, foreign languages, geography, history, and science). With these funds, experts would identify what students should know and be able to do in each subject, and these choices would help each state shape its standards for graduation.

The grants were unsuccessful because the experts produced objectionable products. Congress found the history standards to be too radical in content and pedagogy. Halfway through the grant, the Department of Education judged the English language arts efforts to lack content or actual standards. States rejected the constructivist teaching principles behind the mathematics standards. As a result, federal authorities retreated from providing models for state standards, creating space for private companies and nonprofits to fill the void when the Bush Administration mandated world-class state standards when it reauthorized the ESEA as No Child Left Behind (NCLB).

Basic Skills

A Nation at Risk focused on reform of high schools, assuming that rigorous standards and curriculum would trickle down into the middle and elementary schools. Once high school standards were set for graduation, state curriculum designers would develop lessons that would support students' steady progress toward those ends. Yet efforts to set benchmarks toward graduation demonstrated that many students began high school unprepared to access the new rigorous and rich high school curriculum. Too many could not read, write, or calculate sufficiently to be initiated in the structures and traditions of history, science, or literature. In response, the Department of Education and National Institute of Child and Human Development turned its attention to address basic skills, funding research studies and reports to determine how to improve these prerequisites for a rigorous education.

Becoming a Nation of Readers (Anderson et al., 1985), *Beginning to Read* (Adams, 1990), *Preventing Reading Difficulties in Young Children* (Snow et al., 1998), and, finally, *Teaching Children to Read* (National Reading Panel, 2000) map the route away from the NCEE's recommendation to equip students to comprehend, interpret, evaluate, and use ideas toward preoccupation with students' rudimentary skills of decoding texts quickly and accurately. Discussions concerning the science and methods of beginning reading instruction blocked substantive consideration of what students should read at any grade level. High school reading education of any type was neglected in the NCLB emphasis on the Reading First Initiative.

High-Stakes Testing

A Nation at Risk stated unequivocally that the stakes were high for America unless high schools were reformed. Faced with these facts, the NCEE believed that state and local officials would work diligently to reform high schools in order to educate America properly. Assessments would be necessary to inform daily instruction and to assure that individuals were making measured progress toward rigorous curricular goals. High-stakes examinations would be required only to determine if students had learned enough to merit a diploma. As the 1980s wore on, federal officials began to question the sincerity of state and local efforts to bring about these needed reforms and to ensure that all students were making progress. The George H. W. Bush Administration called for tests at the end of third, fifth, and eighth grades with public reporting of the scores. Although the Bill Clinton administration failed to negotiate the reauthorization of the ESEA at the end of his second term, its proposal included annual testing of all students.

With the reauthorization of ESEA as NCLB in 2002, the George W. Bush Administration mandated that all students would test "proficient" in reading, math, and science by 2014. States would develop federally acceptable state standards, adopt annual tests from third to eighth grades to demonstrate each student's adequate yearly progress toward proficiency, and publish annually the percentages of students scoring at below basic, basic, proficient, or advanced levels on those state tests. To ensure that all groups were treated equally, schools would be required to disaggregate those percentages by race, income level, home language, and ability. Schools that failed repeatedly to produce adequate yearly progress for all groups would be subject to punishments—reduced funding, reorganization as a charter school, or closure. In order to prevent states from cheating this system—accepting poor standards, creating easy tests, or setting low proficiency threshold scores—NCLB required states to participate in the National Assessment of Educational Progress as the national report card. In these ways, test scores alone would determine who was and who was not educated.

Market Orientation

The NCEE defined the American crisis as having an old structure for schooling that could no longer meet the demands of a new economy. Just as different business models were needed for America to compete internationally, different educational models would be necessary. Those different business models uncoupled companies from communities in order to enable production and service to become more flexible and quick to meet market demand and to maximize the profits and dividends. The corporations that supported the NCEE's recommendations in the 1980s—IBM, Xerox, and Kodak, to name a few—were less successful in making this transition than Microsoft, SunAmerica, and Walmart. With profits from their businesses, their owners established foundations to shelter portions of their wealth from taxation and to work for socially beneficial purposes. At the turn of the century, these foundations turned their gaze to public school reform with similar rhetoric as the NCEE, but without an emphasis on past traditions.

Ravitch (2010) labels this group, "the billionaire boys' club," and laments their abilities to intervene in public education at every level from policy right down to classroom practice. The foundations work without public oversight and, therefore, are free to use their funding in order to pursue their private agendas and define them as social good. With little regard for history, tradition, or community, their market strategies—competition, choice, deregulation, incentives, and flexibility—have become driving forces in all aspects of school reform. Ravitch (2010) does not mince words: "With so much money and power aligned against the neighborhood public school and against education as a profession, public education itself is placed at risk" (p. 222).

Conservatives understand poverty as a lack of moral resources to make a good life for oneself and one's family. This lack of resources leads individuals to choose ends that are not valued in the economy and, therefore, to live without the free market providing for their human needs as it does for others who have made different choices. Conservatives believe that families are primarily responsible for developing the moral resources among their children and for insisting that schools build on that foundation. Traditional values and community ties are the rope that makes this net secure. The ability to read is fundamental to developing and using these moral resources to help individuals recognize the connections between their choices and their economic, social, and spiritual well-being. With its moral compass and intellectual challenge, conservative reading education makes community, the economy, and democracy work.

> The ultimate goal is to make sure that young children are exposed to inspiring, demanding works of literature. Good schools don't focus solely on teaching the skills of reading, but also pay attention to what children read and the knowledge that they draw from their books. Keep this thought in mind; education is the architecture of the soul, the leading of children to what is good and fine. Expect your child's English teacher to lead him to truly good and fine works of literature. (Bennett, Finn, & Cribb, 1999, p. 105)

5
COMPETITION
Neoliberals

> The I.T. revolution is giving individuals more and more cheap tools of innovation, collaboration and creativity. . . . And the globalization side of this revolution is integrating more and more of these empowered people into ecosystems, where they can innovate and manufacture more products and services that make people's lives more healthy, educated, entertained, productive, and comfortable. . . .
>
> The best of these ecosystems will be cities and towns that combine a university, an educated populace, a dynamic business community and the fastest broadband connections on earth. . . . The countries that thrive will be those that build more of these towns that make possible high-performance knowledge exchanges and generation. . . .
>
> The more information and trends you mine and analyze, and the more talented human capital, bandwidth and computing power you apply to that data, the more innovation you'll get. . . .
>
> The critical questions for America today have to be how we deploy more ultra-high-speed networks and applications in university towns to invent more high-value-added service and manufactured goods and how we educate more workers to do these jobs—the only way we can maintain the middle class. (Friedman, 2012, A13)

Thomas Friedman's statements are quoted from his *New York Times* op-ed column, "So Much Fun. So Irrelevant," chastising Republican presidential candidates for chattering away during debates about same-sex marriage, gun rights, and taxes. Friedman wanted them to concentrate on "the world in which we're living and how we adapt to it" before it's too late. Although Friedman did not use the term *neoliberal*, he offers many neoliberal values in this argument. Information and communication technology (ICT) has flattened "the world in which we're living," providing faster and cheaper tools with which anyone anywhere can innovate, collaborate, and create. Everyone, everywhere is, therefore, in competition with each other in order to prosper (to at least "maintain a middle class").

Accordingly, each must understand herself or himself as an entrepreneur and manage her or his life accordingly. Among other traits, this means imagining how each can prepare to find new opportunities for profit and reward by moving herself or himself, collaborators, and society forward. The most fortunate empowered entrepreneurs live in countries that devote substantial resources in order to organize digitally connected nodes with smart tools, smart people, and smart markets. In these environments, entrepreneurs use tools to collect, sift, mine, and analyze big data for "new inventions in health care, education, manufacturing, and retailing." More smart ecosystems are better than fewer, bigger datasets are better than smaller, and faster is better than slower in this competition of all against all.

Beyond the fastest broadband connections on Earth, the organization of "high performance knowledge exchanges and generation" requires governments to provide incentives for empowered people to congregate and take risks—a trade regime that protects infant industries; a financial system that provides for patent capitalization; good bankruptcy laws to protect capitalists and a good social safety net to support workers through times of transition; and public subsidies for research, development, and training. Once in place, the government steps aside to let the markets work.

Although some smart ecosystems have emerged in America—"Silicon Valley, Austin, Boulder, Cambridge, and Ann Arbor"—Friedman doubts America's resolve to adapt to this reality because politics-as-usual keeps legislators' and public attention on the wrong priorities. Conservatives worry about cultural issues and liberals worry about equity, while global competition overtakes America's 20th-century world advantages. In Friedman's words, both positions might be "entertaining," but they are "irrelevant" because "right now . . . America is focused too much on getting 'average' bandwidth to the last 5 percent of the country in rural areas, rather than getting ultra-high-speed bandwidth to the top 5 percent in university towns, who will invent the future." Friedman warns that America follows this equity path at its peril because the smart ecosystems are "the job factories of the future."

Because "this is the world in which we are living," Friedman offers technical suggestions for how "we adapt to it" and not philosophical debate. There is no time to fret whether this version of a wireless world is good or bad or somewhere in between, he tells us. Rather, Americans need to act now because "this *is* the world." That means readjusting American priorities away from immediate equity of access to outmoded technology and toward effective and efficient adaptation to this world of continuous global competition. The federal government must address two issues: It must decide how to facilitate and expand the creation of smart ecosystems through connection to the fastest broadband available (and be prepared to continuously update that capacity), and it must choose how to retool its education system in order to create "workers for the jobs" in and around these environments. The more educated the worker, the more ecosystems can innovate. The more innovation, the more prosperous a country can become.

The neoliberal representation of poverty is implied in Friedman's argument. For a variety of reasons, the poor lack the human capital to attract sufficient income to sustain themselves or their families in a rapidly changing world. Perhaps they live in a society that doesn't recognize the world in which we live and, therefore, the poor are limited in their abilities to position themselves well within the global competition. Or perhaps the institutions within their society do not or cannot provide sufficient support to facilitate smart ecosystems in order to maintain a middle class. Both of these reasons echo liberal explanations of poverty—through no fault of their own, the poor are denied access to the means to prepare themselves to make and sustain themselves in making adequate incomes. The government, then, has some role to play in fighting poverty.

Yet, Friedman also points toward individuals who choose not to acknowledge or adapt to this change in reality (in his case, Republican presidential candidates during a debate), and therefore freely pursue life goals other than economic sustainability. This is a conservative take on poverty. Poor individuals choose traditions, culture, and faith over developing their human capital sufficiently in order to maintain their economic well-being when innovation makes their skills and knowledge obsolete. Because of those choices, the poor or soon-to-be poor elect candidates who they believe will protect their liberties, but who are unwilling to make the needed changes to save many from poverty. In the global innovation economy, those choices mean the American standard of living will necessarily decline. The school curriculum has two roles to play in fighting poverty, then. First, it must develop a realist worldview among citizens, and, second, it must produce workers with the capacities to create and maintain these ecosystems.

Government policies and school curricula cannot prevent poverty by themselves, Friedman argues, because they are not sufficiently flexible to meet the rapidly changing conditions in the global innovation economy. Only a free market economy can organize the empowered entrepreneurs into highly productive innovative systems in order to supply for human needs. When nurtured by government policies and school curriculum, those systems become the job factories of the future, providing goods, services, and incomes to sustain and grow the American middle class. The market, then, is the neoliberal answer to fighting poverty.

Neoliberals frame poverty as a social problem (and not just a personal choice) because it wastes resources, undermining the productivity of a community, state, or nation. National prosperity rests on the productive capacity of its citizens and, therefore, the poor deserve short-term support to provide time and opportunity for them to acquire the new skills and knowledge necessary to gain productive employment. Current liberal policies based on the New Deal and the

Great Society, providing long-term aid for food, shelter, health care, and income, divert valuable government resources that would be better invested in production and maintenance of the conditions for innovation. Without that investment, the American economy declines, hurting members of the middle class, working class, and the poor. And because the productive capacities of individuals multiply through their smart organization in ecosystems—making all within a country dependent on all others—neoliberals cannot honor the conservative position to let the poor be free to live according to their personal choice. To win in the global competition, all Americans must realize their full productive potential.

In this chapter I describe neoliberal reading education and its relationship to poverty, connect the relationship to neoliberal values, and present a neoliberal thread in education policy from the *A Nation at Risk* report to Race to the Top. Neoliberalism lacks a declaration of sentiments such as *The Sharon Statement* or the legacy of the New Deal or the Great Society. Few call themselves neoliberals, yet many in power act according to its principles. The ideology has formed around the pursuit of liberal goals—individual liberty, equality before the law, and protection of property—using market relations, rather than government policies, uniting some liberals disillusioned with big government and libertarian conservatives. Neoliberal reading education faces the uncertain future of global competition by attempting to harness and extend liberals' equal opportunity to "best practices" of teaching and conservatives' effort to grasp the structures and codes of traditional academic disciplines in order to prepare American students to compete and win in the global innovation economy. To accomplish this goal, neoliberal legislators, pundits, and educators have proposed policies that would unify educational efforts across state lines, enabling smart educational ecosystems to mine and analyze "big data" to discover more effective and efficient trends in teaching every student to read.

Neoliberal Reading Education

Universal Preschool Education

> So, tonight, I propose working with states to make high-quality preschool available to every single child in America. That's something we should be able to do. (President Obama, February 12, 2013, State of the Union Address)

With this proposal, President Obama pushes Friedman's call for educational reform into the first five years of childhood. Obama's logic goes something like this: Americans are not ready for the global innovation economy because public schools do not prepare students adequately for the rapid changes, and schools cannot prepare students adequately because too many American children are not ready for the school curriculum when they start kindergarten. This thinking troubles both the typical liberal and conservative responses because neither the federal governments' existing program—Head Start—nor individual families and private preschools have been equal to the task. Innovation is needed, and the President proposed a policy that would provide opportunities for all four-year-old Americans to attend a high-quality preschool program.

President Obama hypothesizes, and certainly he's not alone, that attending systematically to preschool children's physical, emotional, social, cultural, and academic development will increase their chances of school and life success. He argues that studies show that graduates of high-quality preschools are "more likely to read and do math at grade level, graduate from high school, hold a job, and form more stable families of their own" than those children who lack such experiences. Hypothesis and argument are not enough to enact policy, however; legislators and officials must also understand the proposed action as politically acceptable and economically feasible. Obama's politics for his proposal are captured in two metaphors from the previous quote. "Working with" implies collaboration in which states propose models that meet federal high-quality benchmarks in order to qualify for substantial federal funding ($75 billion over 10 years). "Available to" promises benefits to all American families, not just those children eligible for Head Start. While the President admits that the project would be expensive, he reported: "Every dollar we invest in high-quality early childhood education can save more than seven dollars later on."

Obama used a variety of sources to provide his evidence to support this proposal. His point of departure—that too few American children are prepared for schooling—came from the Organization of Economic Cooperation and Development (2012), which ranks the United States 28th among 38 developed countries for the share of four-year-olds enrolled in high-quality programs (less than 30 percent). He explained: "Most middle class parents can't afford a few hundred bucks a week for private preschool, and for poor kids who need help the most, this lack of access to preschool education can shadow them for the rest of their lives." He named Georgia and Oklahoma as states already providing this service successfully. His return-on-investment statistic referenced the Perry School Project from the 1960s and a study that followed 123 African American graduates and members of the control group for over 40 years (Heckman, Moon, Pinto, Savelyev, & Yavitz, 2010). Conspicuous by its absence was any mention of Head Start, the federal government's existing program for four-year-olds. Two months before the State of the Union Address, the federal government released the *Third Grade Follow-up to the Head Start Impact Study, Final Report,* which concluded: "By the end of 3rd grade, there were very few impacts in any of the four domains of cognitive, social-emotional, health and parenting practices" (Head Start, 2012, p. xvii). Obama didn't mention Head Start because it had been found not to be high quality.

As critics and supporters were quick to identify, the President's evidence does not align easily. The Georgia and Oklahoma programs were too new to track any data on graduation rates, jobs, or families. Their impact on achievement was modest—a point or two on the National Assessment of Education Progress tests at fourth grade—and states without universal preschools (Massachusetts, Kentucky, and others) outperformed Georgia and Oklahoma (when adjusted for demographic differences). Strong long-term effects were only documented in the Perry School Project and the Carolina Abecedarian Project, which were two-year programs with per-pupil costs of $19,000 and $95,000, respectively. In Georgia, data suggested the best outcomes were for "disadvantaged children residing in small towns and rural areas" (FactCheck.org, 2013). Yet, Head Start, the program design for that target group, showed few lasting results. Obama's spin on the evidence during his address led Grover ("Russ") Whitehurst, former head of the federal Institute of Education Sciences, to opine: "The administration has been marketing its plan with about the same amount of balance that any large business brings to the task of selling a new product in which it is heavily invested, which is to say that it is putting forward the best possible case" (Whitehurst, 2013).

Obama's proposal, then, rested on speculation that high-quality, cost-efficient, universal programs could be developed through a federal partnership with states that avoids the pitfalls of Head Start. According to the White House factsheet on the plan ("President Obama's Plan," 2013), in order to access federal funding, states would meet quality benchmarks—statewide standards for early learning; well-prepared, engaged teachers; small class sizes; a rigorous, intentional, research-based curriculum; comprehensive health and social services; and plans for effective evaluation and review of programs. Qualifying states would, then, be free to distribute federal and matching state funds to any program that agreed to these conditions and would submit its student data for statewide and national analyses in order to determine which programs or parts of programs deliver the best short-term, achievement test, and life-long results. In this way, each program (including local Head Start programs) would compete with all others to connect its high-quality inputs directly to students' high-quality outcomes.

Friedman's concerns and market solutions converge in President Obama's proposal for universal preschool. Moving to a national scale, the preschool market becomes large and lucrative enough to attract the attention of innovators, who are free from commitments to communities or established bureaucracies and care only for systems that work. By "mining and analyzing" the evaluative data from high-quality preschools across the country, more innovation toward better outcomes becomes not only possible but likely. By sharing the evaluations and innovations with the public, the market prepares parents to choose wisely among preschools, providing strong incentives for preschools to improve service and outcomes while chasing mediocre and poor programs from the field of early childhood education. With modest support from government, then, the market crafts a more dynamic early education system that can shift with future changes and find solutions to school readiness, improving the lives of the poor, lower-, and middle-class citizens now and in the future. In a sense, then, Whitehurst was correct about Obama's pitch.

His proposal for universal preschool was a business plan inviting capitalization—a plan that could return up to 700 percent profit within a generation.

21st-Century Schooling

The neoliberal push for educational reform doesn't stop with preschool. If America is to win in the global innovation economy, then the organizational form, the disposition of teachers, and the substance of "public schooling" must change and change quickly. "We have to get better faster than ever before at education" (Duncan, 2011). Neoliberals argue that the current American school system is the wrong tool to win the future. That system was designed to meet the demands of an industrial world in which stable communities produced goods and services for regional, state, and national markets. Those schools educated workers with the dispositions and skill sets to meet industrial demands. Since World War II, however, markets have become global and are rapidly changing, requiring workers with new flexible dispositions and the capacity to continuously update their human capital. Despite constant attention from sincere American school reformers, neoliberals contend that the old industrial design has not and cannot meet 21st-century demands. America needs a new education system, and like Friedman demanded in his editorial, America needs educational leaders who will concentrate on the "world in which we're living and how we adapt to it."

Ken Robinson (2010) argues that the current system alienates and dulls the creativity of many students through its organizational structure. Although we are living in a remarkably stimulating world with technology enabling global communication, we conceive of schooling as something that happens within a self-contained box in each community that can meet all students' needs. Although new business values collaboration and innovation, schools still separate students by their age, sort information into abstract disciplines, and affix skills and facts to students as each age cohort moves through the system. Each student receives the standard academic package and learns and is assessed individually, at the same time each day, and across the same period each year. Although the economy seeks entrepreneurship and creativity, Robinson concludes that the American school system produces conformity, compliance, and standardization among graduates, and then sends them ill-prepared into an economy "to innovate and manufacture more products and services that make people's lives more healthy, educated, entertained, productive, and comfortable" (Friedman, 2012).

Current school reforms fail, Frederick Hess (2010) diagnosed, because educational leaders and the public cling to three assumptions about education: (1) They assume that schooling should bring uniform outcomes for all students because everyone can and should reach the same standards, (2) they assume that there is one best system that will work for all students under all circumstances, and (3) they assume that public education must be government-run in order to ensure equity. Hess argued that the first two assumptions misrepresent human potential and diversity. The first implies that we already know what all people should know in order to invent the future, and the second suggests that we know precisely how each should learn that content. Hess states that we know neither the *what* nor the *how* for all students, and that American schools prove just that annually. The third assumption, he suggested, ignores the documented successes of the public/private partnerships already established in building America's infrastructure, providing emergency services, and maintaining national security.

> Instead of expending more and more time seeking the one best way to educate all children, the path out of this tangled thicket lies in defining an essential *minimalist* body of skills and knowledge for all students and then taking care to avoid prescriptions about methods or content beyond that floor. (Hess, 2010, p. 129)

Heeding his caution to avoid prescription, Hess echoes Friedman in his suggestions. He's not interested in forcing change; rather, he seeks to unbundle education from schools-as-we-know-them, making them simply one option among many. Hess sees the information technology revolution as providing new tools to disrupt entrenched routines, to leverage expertise, and to end the tyranny of zip-code schooling. After the revamped schools have secured that every student has acquired the essential body of skills and knowledge, they can serve as brokers for independent instructional services, coordinating stand-alone providers in order to customize what students learn each day. The well-to-do already enjoy such services, Hess maintains, purchasing effective extracurricular instruction for their children in arts, athletics, and academics. School for One, Tutor.com, and Smarthinking defy geography, he adds, making such services available digitally. He concludes that government funding for per-pupil vouchers would simply democratize these advantages. Access to information and market forces would ensure quality control as it does in other public/private services already, and performance assessments (instead of standardized high-stakes testing) would keep learners and providers accountable.

Beyond the form of schooling, neoliberals seek to overhaul its substance as well. Since the early 1990s (Marshall & Tucker, 1992) neoliberals have asked: What are the essential skills and knowledge student/workers need in order to adapt quickly to "the world in which we are living"? Who needs these skills and knowledge? How will we know when students have acquired them? At present, neoliberals promote two slightly competitive, largely compatible alternatives to curricular reform—the Common Core State Standards (CCS) and the Partnership for 21st Century Skills (P21; 2013). Both address more than English language arts and seek to change daily classroom activities by setting standards.

The CCS movement began at the 1996 National Education Summit when representatives of the National Governors Association (NGA), philanthropic foundations, and business established Achieve, a nongovernmental agency, to broker support for rigorous high school graduation requirements. Achieve identified and articulated the problems clearly: 70 percent of high school graduates needed remedial help in college, fewer than half left college with a degree, more than 60 percent of employers reported that high school graduates lacked basic skills, and the majority of workers believed high school did not prepare them adequately for work. By 2004 Achieve presented high school graduation benchmarks based on "the knowledge and skills that colleges and employers actually expect, if young people are to succeed in their institutions" (Achieve, 2004, p. 3). If implemented, all high school graduates would demonstrate mastery through both completion of enhanced course work and standards-based tests. In English language arts, graduates would surpass benchmarks organized in eight strands: Language (7 benchmarks), Communications (7), Writing (10), Research (5), Logic (9), Information Text (11), Media (4), and Literature (9). For example,

. . . high school graduates can:

> Research D1—Define and narrow a problem or research topic (p. 34);
> Logic E1—distinguish among facts and opinions, evidence and inferences (p. 34);
> Informational Text F1—follow instructions in informational or technical texts to perform specific tasks, answer questions or solve problems (p. 35);
> Literature H1—demonstrate knowledge of 18th and 19th century foundational works of American literature. (p. 37)

In 2009 the NGA and the Council of Chief State School Officers (CCSSO) hired Achieve to translate its graduation benchmarks for English language arts into a K–12 common core standards template that states could choose as a pattern for their state standards. Achieve brought in David Coleman, CEO of Student Achievement Partners, to direct the English language arts translation. Through a series of meetings with selected panels of experts, consultations with states, and one public hearing, the final version of the template was produced within 12 months and, according to NGA and CCSSO's Common Core Validation Committee (2010), "unlike past standards-setting efforts, the Common Core State Standards are based on best practices in national and international education, as well as research and input from numerous sources" (p. 4). The Common Core Standards for English language arts have been adopted in 46 states in order to be implemented in 2014.

In the process of translation, Achieve's benchmarks were reorganized into eight categories: anchor; reading literature; reading information text; reading foundational skills; writing; speaking and listening; language; and range, quality, and complexity. The 10 anchor standards—the competencies that high school graduates will possess—were organized into four categories (Key Ideas and Details, Craft and Structure, Integration of Knowledge and Ideas, and Range of Reading and Level of Text Complexity). For example:

> CCSS.ELA-Literacy.CCRA.R.1 Reading closely to determine what the text says explicitly and to make logical inferences from it; cite specific textual evidence when writing or speaking to support conclusions drawn from the text.
> CCSS>ELA-Literacy CCRA.R.4 Interpret words and phrases as they are used in a text, including determining technical, connotative, and figurative meanings, and analyze how specific word choices shape meaning and tone.
> CCSS>ELA-Literacy.CCRA.R.7 Integrate and evaluate content presented in diverse media and formats including visually and quantitatively, as well as in words.
> CCSS>ELA-Literacy.CCRA.R.10 Read and comprehend complex literary and informational texts independently and proficiently.

Starting from the anchor standards, Common Core committees used reverse design principles, research, and judgment to identify the sequence of enabling standards that would ensure students' graduation and success in a career or college. Under Coleman's direction, the committee wrote standards for each of eight categories from kindergarten to 12th grade. Coleman explains that the CCS make six fundamental shifts from previous state standards (Coleman, 2012). In order to ensure that all students develop appropriate vocabulary and informational capital, students will read equal amounts of informational and literary texts. This will encourage elementary school teachers to teach science and history regularly. Second, in middle and high schools, reading and writing standards will be spread among all subject teachers—English, social studies, and science—in order to capture the different logics and genres from different disciplines. Third, the standards will require mastery of more complex texts as students move from primary to intermediate, middle, and then high school grades, ensuring that graduates will be ready for the complex texts of college and careers. Fourth, teachers across the grades will take a developmental approach to the close reading of texts in which readers will first discover the meaning within a text before they begin to render opinions of its value. Fifth, in all subjects, students will be encouraged to use evidence to make appropriate arguments complete with textual references, and, then, to communicate complex information clearly. Finally, special attention will be devoted to the development of a rich academic vocabulary composed of content terms in each discipline and structural words that unite them in research and analysis (e.g., hypothesis, axiom, generalization). Coleman argues that this last step is essential for low-income and English language learners who do not encounter such words often outside of school.

Conservatives and liberals are guarded in their approaches to the Common Core. Diane Ravitch (2010) applauds the rigor within the standards and its respect for teachers—"these standards will establish *what* students need to learn, but they will not dictate *how* teachers should teach" (Common Core State Standards Initiative, 2010). She worries, however, about their private funding and sparse reading lists. Anthony Petrosky (2012) scolds educators who fear the attention to detail and text within close reading, explaining that words, evidence, and argument figure prominently in every learned explanation of academic literacy. Yet, he thinks the official published and digital exemplars overemphasize linear reading of important text from words to central ideas and limit teachers' pedagogical imaginations of how close reading might be taught and learned. Robert Calfee (2013) welcomes the emphasis on reading comprehension throughout the grades, but laments the continued overreliance on the National Reading Panel Report for early literacy learning. Elfrieda Hiebert and Katie Van Sluys (2013) appreciate the attention to text in the standards, yet worry that the official formula for text complexity forces steps too steep for most elementary and middle school readers to climb. P. David Pearson (2013) is encouraged by the sophisticated theoretical representation of comprehension in the categories organizing the anchor standards—key ideas and details (what a text says), craft and structure (what it means), and integrations of knowledge (what it does). However, he argues that the reverse design lacks empirical evidence for the positioning of enabling standards and for the promise that they will lead to mastery of the anchor standards. Although Karen Wixson (2012) values the shifts on the proposed standards-based tests that include texts worth reading, tasks worthy of engagement, and integrated English language arts, she warns that the tests will tax many students' reading abilities and stamina.

Her concern seems prescient. For various reasons, Kentucky and New York administered the Common Core tests in 2012–2013—a year before the curriculum designed to address the standards was fully implemented. Kentucky hired Pearson Inc. to develop a state exam—the Kentucky Performance Rating of Educational Progress—and required students in Grades 3–8 to complete it. The percentage of students scoring "proficient" or better declined by one-third from rates on the previous state reading tests from percentages in the 70s to the 40s (Ujufusa, 2012). In 2013 New York administered one of the two official Common Core tests competing for state adoptions and found that only 31 percent of "students in third through eighth grades met or exceeded the proficiency standard in language arts" ("New York's Common Core Test Scores," 2013, A13). In economically segregated upstate cities, percentages of proficient readers "fell into the single digits." Advocates suggest that these test results demonstrate the need for the common core.

> If the U.S. is to continue to lead the world in economic growth—and the innovation that feeds such growth—we must start, at the very bottom, to

demand more from our students, parents, and educators across all localities, regardless of race, income or geography. (Crotty, 2013)

The Partnership for 21st Century Skills was formed in 2002 as a nongovernmental agency with the support of the federal Department of Education, the National Education Association, and seven information communications technology firms. The P21 mission is to change public school curriculum and pedagogy in order to ensure that graduates will be prepared to create and fill jobs in the global innovation economy. Beyond enhanced traditional curriculum, P21 seeks "to infuse the 3 Rs with the 4 Cs" (critical thinking, communication, creativity, and collaboration). After a decade, the partnership has grown to 36 companies (from Adobe to Walt Disney), 18 states (Arizona to Wisconsin), and most professional teacher organizations (art to science). Other measures of its success are its part in the formation of the bipartisan Congressional 21st Century Skills Caucus in 2011, its authorship of Senate Bill 1483 to provide federal matching funds to states and schools that implement a 21st-century curriculum, and the fact that the P21 founder, Ken Kay, participated in the development of the Republican party platform for the 2012 elections.

The P21 project is based on its *Framework for 21st Century Learning,* a design to augment traditional student outcomes and school support systems through increased use of:

Smart tools (digital information, communication technology hardware and software);
Interdisciplinary themes (global awareness; financial literacy; civic literacy, health literacy, and environmental literacy); and
Three 21st century skill sets:

1. Learning and Innovation—creativity and innovation, critical thinking and problem solving, communication, and collaboration;
2. Information, Media, and Technology—informational literacy, media literacy, and ICT literacy; and
3. Life and Career—flexibility and adaptability, initiative and self-direction, social and cultural skills, productivity and accountability, and leadership and responsibility.

To support teachers as they make these changes, P21 provides two documents and a series of video examples.

The *P21/Common Core Tool Kit* refers to literacy frequently—listing seven types of literacy in its global themes and new skill sets—but never defines literacy explicitly. Literacy seems to be a student's control of the code, logic, and information within the broad (literacy) types. P21 assumes that Common Core will deliver print literacy in ways that will enable graduates to compete in the global innovation economy, but doubts the transfer of these skills to other media and technologies without specific demonstrations and instruction. Moreover, P21 understands the CCS as too traditional to develop nonacademic skill sets necessary for the competitions among Friedman's ecosystems. P21 intends to equip schools (in whatever forms they might take) to add value to student human capital by featuring the use of smart tools, combining traditional academic subjects in order to address authentic contemporary theme issues, and encouraging the four Cs and the life and career skill set.

In conjunction with the National Council of Teachers of English, P21 provides the *English Language Arts Curricular Skills Map* to help English language arts teachers imagine how the Framework could produce workable curricula and lessons. P21 lists about 100 brief examples at the 4th-, 8th-, and 12th-grade levels. For instance, in order to develop students' creativity and innovation, teachers could implement the following:

> 4th grade—Read several trickster stories and watch several cartoons, and then write an original tale, presenting it to others through stop-motion or claymation films.
> 8th grade—Read the poem "Where I'm From" and the contemporary song with the same title, and then write a poem based on your background. Create a webpage for the poem with hyperlinks to photographs, illustrations, and other texts that enhance or explain your intended meaning. After viewing others' poem webpages, link to three other sites with brief explanations for your choice of connections.
> 12th grade—After reading a dystopian novel, create a movie trailer that highlights universal questions raised in the novel. View other's trailers and write a script for an "At the Movies" review panel.

The P21 map matrix covers the 12 particulars of three new 21st-century skill sets, touching on each of the interdisciplinary global themes. For example, fourth-grade teachers might encourage critical thinking and problem solving within financial literacy by having their students review proposals at a microfinancing website, and then research and report on the economic and social impact of a proposal. After each report has been presented, the class would choose one proposal and "create an appropriate activity to raise money to support the chosen project." Eighth-grade English teachers developing students' informational and health literacies simultaneously could complete a literature circle unit of teen problem novels, having students compose a list of significant social, emotional, and health issues that teens face today. Working in groups, students would research one issue in order to create a public service announcement to persuade their peers to take appropriate action and present it on a school's closed YouTube channel.

P21 projects and curricula address Friedman's challenges explicitly, developing a realist global awareness through mastery of financial, civic, health, and environmental uses of literacy. Where the P21 framework is deployed, students are expected to master skills to obtain, access, and manage information accurately and efficiently using ICT tools in order to analyze data and to communicate their findings to others effectively. Their performances of these worldly, in-class projects will attest to their development toward mastery of the four Cs and ICT skill sets that employers desire, and will later materialize in higher scores on the international tests that prize solving ill-defined problems (Kay, 2010). At the same time, students develop the appropriate dispositions through demonstrations of mastery of life and career skill sets, learning to monitor themselves within rapid changes to economies, governments, health care, and the environment in order to be creative, innovative, flexible, adaptable, self-directed, productive, and accountable when in or between times of learning. In the end, P21 literacy education is designed to produce more American citizens who better understand the world in which we're living and how to adapt to it.

Neoliberal reading education does not target the poor for special educational treatment because the economy demands that most Americans improve their literacy skills significantly and continuously. Schools as we know them and reading curricula as currently practiced have been unable to adapt to this demand because liberal and conservative educational leaders look to the past in order to address the future. For all to be served fairly, reading standards must be raised and directed toward the work already taking place in the dynamic economic ecosystems that Friedman describes, and reading education must become unbound from institutional traditions in order to invite and enable innovation. To do that, markets and competition must be introduced and coupled with the generation of big data. Empowered educational entrepreneurs will then mine and analyze reading education information and trends in order to design custom programs to deliver the Common Core and P21 standards to all.

Neoliberal Reading Education Policy

During the 2010 NGA meeting in Washington, D.C., President Obama offered the official rationale for the Common Core Standards.

> [Asian nations] want their kids to excel because they understand that whichever country out-educates the other is going to out-compete us in the future. So that's what we're up against. That's what's at stake—nothing less than our primacy in the world. . . . And I want to commend all of you for acting collectively through the National Governors Association to develop common academic standards that will better position our students for success. (Obama, 2010)

And at the 2009 National Conference of State Legislatures in Philadelphia, Bill Gates explained how the standards would do their work.

> Identifying common standards is just the starting point. We'll only know if this effort has succeeded, when the curriculum and the tests are aligned to these standards. Secretary of Education Arne Duncan recently announced that $350 million of the stimulus package will be used to create just these kinds of tests—next generation assessments aligned with the common core. When the tests are aligned with the common standards, the curriculum will line up as well, and it will unleash a powerful market of people providing services for better teaching. For the first time, there will be a large uniform base of customers looking at using products that can help every kid learn and every teacher get better. (Gates, 2009)

Competition is the engine in both these statements. As Friedman argued, competition at the global level defines the world. President Obama suggests that education or the continuous development of human capital is a primary piston in that engine, and he argues that Asian educational engineers have that piston firing more effectively and more efficiently than American educational experts. Raising standards to international levels and then distributing those standards across the states, he believes, should make Americans, and therefore the American economy, more competitive. And even during the Great Recession, President Obama was willing to devote considerable government resources to build a competitive educational system.

Gates positions the new generation of reading tests as the means with which to judge individuals', schools', states' and the nation's potential, signaling several levels of competition to qualify for roles within the existing and emerging smart economic ecosystems. The national scope of the Common Core project and its identified measures, Gates explains, invite entrepreneurs with their ICT tools to mine data and to innovate in order to increase the human capital of all teachers and students. The road to arrive at this promised neoliberal triumph must pass through state control of education with its local monopolies over schooling and its systems for training and retaining teachers.

Changing the Form of Schools

Charter schools are independent public schools that are organized and run according to their performance contracts. They are considered to be public schools because they are tuition free, open admission, publicly funded, and accountable for state and federal academic standards. Charter schools are independent because their "charters," and not existing state and local regulations, detail their school mission, program, target enrollment, performance goals, and methods of assessment. Families choose to send their children to charter schools rather than to attend the local school to which they would be assigned. Although free from some federal, state, and local regulation, charter schools remain responsible for students' academic achievement, sound fiscal management, and organizational stability. Any nonsectarian individual or group can apply for a charter—parents, community leaders, entrepreneurs, businesses, teachers, school districts, and even municipalities. In these ways, charter schools respond to neoliberal concerns to provide innovative models for 21st-century public schools.

In 1991 Minnesota enacted the first charter school law, inviting a limited number of break-the-mold schools to be created. After the federal Public School Redefinition Act failed to provide direct federal grants to initiate charters, state legislatures passed a diverse array of charter school laws with differing regulations concerning the number of charters allowed, the possibility of virtual schools, the authorizing agencies, and whether charter school teachers were to be covered by collective bargaining agreements. In 2013 charter schools serve approximately 4 percent of the nation's public school students with over two million students in 6,000 schools across 41 states. Between 2009 and 2013 charter school enrollments increased 80 percent, and most significantly among Black and Hispanic students living below the official poverty line. According to the Institute of Education Science, most charter schools operate in urban areas (55 percent urban, 21 percent suburbs, 8 percent small towns, and 16 percent rural areas). Most provide services for elementary school–aged students (54 percent elementary, 27 percent secondary, and 19 percent combined). Forty-eight percent enroll both middle- and mixed-income students—19 percent have few poor students and 33 percent have mostly poor students enrolled.

The boldest experiment with charter school state policy remade the New Orleans public school system in 2005 after Hurricane Katrina. At that time, Louisiana Governor Kathleen Blanco stated: "I know this is a once-in-a-lifetime opportunity. Now is the time to act, now is the time to think out of the box and now is the time to turn a failing school system into a model for the nation" (as quoted in Robelen, 2005). Education consultant Paul Hill (2005) labeled New Orleans a "greenfield"—a large urban public school system to be built from scratch. State Act 35 enabled the Louisiana department of education to assume control of 102 of the 117 city schools in order to create a blended system. Fifteen schools remained under the Orleans Parish School District control, and 102 became charter schools in the state-run Recovery District with decentralized authority over mission, program, and assessment. All hurricane-displaced teachers were fired in 2005 with the option to reapply for jobs within the new district. In 2013, 80 percent of New Orleans public school students attend charters, and according to the Center for Research on Education Outcomes' (CREDO) National Charter School Study 2013, half of the city's charter schools outperform traditional public schools in reading.

The CREDO 2013 study updates its 2009 findings that students attending charter schools did not fare as well on reading tests as students attending traditional public schools. One recommendation of that first report was for states to be more vigilant in revoking charters from schools that do not achieve their mission. The 2013 study examined the performance of charter schools in 26 states (that accounted for over 90 percent of the students attending charters) and found that the neoliberal experiment of providing competition for public schools was beginning to work with a shift toward better quality. According to the new report, 25 percent of charter schools produced significantly higher reading test scores than traditional counterparts, 56 percent showed no difference, and 19 percent performed significantly lower. Among the various groups of charter school students, poor students benefited the most when compared to their traditional public school peers. On May 7, 2012, President Obama proclaimed National Charter Schools Week.

> Whether created by parents and teachers or community and civic leaders, charter schools serve as incubators of innovation in neighborhoods across our country. These institutions give educators the freedom to cultivate new teaching models and develop creative methods to meet students' needs. This unique flexibility is matched by strong accountability and high standards, so underperforming charter schools can be closed, while those that consistently help students succeed can serve as models of reform for other public schools. (Obama, 2012)

Changing Teachers' Dispositions

In order to unbundle education from schooling, neoliberal school reformers seek to transform teachers' dispositions. As Robinson and Hess explained, the 20th-century model of schooling cannot meet the demands of a 21st-century education. Those 20th-century assumptions, regulations, and routines must be disrupted, they argue, if students are to develop their human capital sufficiently to earn a sustainable position in the global innovation economy. This is particularly true in schools enrolling low-income and poor students who have been and remain poorly served in traditional public schools. Changing a school's charter or mission invites change, but school personnel must believe in and act on those invitations. To address this issue, neoliberals work to influence teachers' dispositions through training and retention policies. Innovative policies lead the way.

Teach for America (TFA) was first proposed as a Peace Corps–like organization that would provide educational supports for low-income communities. Recent college graduates would volunteer to teach for two years in urban and rural communities that suffer from teacher shortages, bringing their idealistic commitment and demonstrated subject-area knowledge to schools in order to change students' life chances. The proposal garnered immediate support from several philanthropic foundations and enthusiastic endorsements from the *New York Times* and

Newsweek, and in 1990 TFA selected its first cohort of 500 ivy-league graduates for this mission. After five weeks of "boot camp" teacher training, the volunteers took their places in classrooms as regular teachers with salaries and benefits according to district contracts and a small stipend from TFA to spend on professional development. When recruits completed their commitments, TFA founders assumed that they would form the nucleus of a new movement of education leaders, pushing school reform agendas that would bypass colleges of education and teacher unions. TFA's 20th-year reunion was held in Washington, D.C., celebrating growth to nearly 50,000 applications each year for approximately 4,500 placements. Despite empirical comparison, which demonstrated that TFA teachers are not as effective at teaching reading as traditionally prepared beginning teachers (Heillig & Jez, 2010), President Obama sent video congratulations.

Two graduates of the first TFA cohort founded the Knowledge Is Power Program (KIPP) in 1994 with public and private funding. It has become the nation's largest charter school network with over 140 schools serving low-income communities with preschool through high school instruction. KIPP recruits its teachers from other schools, recent college graduates, career changers, and TFA alumni and supports their continued development through KIPP Share (an online platform) and KIPP School Summit (an annual week-long gathering of "learning and community-building"). In 2013 President Clinton spoke at the Summit. Curto, Fryer, and Howard (2011) label KIPP a highly effective No Excuses model with "highly aggressive human capital strategies; extended school days or school years; a high level of commitment from students, parents, and faculty; and use of data-driven instruction" (p. 483). The no-excuses metaphor is built on KIPP's culture of personal responsibility. Students', parents', and teachers' dedication and hard work can overcome any barrier to students learning. Students must commit to a code of behavior and regime of study, parents must sign contracts to ensure their child's commitment and to devote time and energy to support the school requirements, and teachers must dedicate themselves to doing whatever it takes in terms of time and teaching in order to raise students' test scores. The aggressive human capital strategies include termination from KIPP schools if dedication, hard work, and higher test scores are not forthcoming.

One observable change in these programs is the movement toward shorter, more intensive teaching careers. Teachers working in the largest charter school network average between two (TFA) and four (KIPP) years of service in the classroom (Rich, 2013). The founder of TFA explained: "The strongest schools develop their teachers tremendously so they become great in the classroom even in their first and second year" (as quoted in Rich, 2013). For example, YES Prep, operator of 13 No Excuses schools nationally, offers new teachers two-and-one-half weeks of training in the summer, daily visits from an administrator, and bi-monthly sessions with instructional coaches to learn classroom management routines, time management, and lesson planning. YES Prep teachers are prepared to devote longer hours in the school day (all teachers are assigned a cell phone to answer any student call for homework assistance until 9:00 p.m. Sunday through Thursday). They employ uniform behavioral reinforcement techniques (classroom celebrations are "two claps and then a sizzle"), and best instructional practices (each skill is taught to mastery and then on to the next skill in the official sequence) during a shorter teaching career. The senior vice president of people and programs at YES Prep paraphrased her mobile teachers and thinking: "O. K., I've got this [teaching], what's the next thing?" (as quoted in Rich, 2013).

A second change is to focus teachers' attention more exclusively on student achievement. As part of the American Recovery and Reinvestment Act of 2009, President Obama sponsored Race to the Top, a $4.35 billion competition among states to encourage innovation and neoliberal reform in public schools. Forty states submitted proposals to win between $20 and $700 million based on their school populations. According to the proposal criteria, winning states would accept the Common Core standards, loosen restrictions on charter schools, establish big data systems, and evaluate teachers and principals with systems based at least in part on student test scores. In 2010 Delaware and Tennessee won in the first round of evaluations. Secretary of Education Arne Duncan (2012) praised the progress in Tennessee: "The report found that after one year [of an evaluation system based on test scores], Tennessee's students made their biggest single-year jump in achievement ever recorded in the state." And later, he praised Tennessee's new policy to base teacher certification on candidates' effects on student achievement during their school internships (Duncan, 2013).

Changing School Substance

Throughout the process of developing the Common Core standards, the NGA and the CCSSO insisted that the federal government "had no role in the development of the common core state standards and will not have a role in their implementation" (Common Core State Standards Initiative, 2013). Despite the protection of the original Elementary and Secondary Education Act (ESEA) legislation preventing the federal government's involvement in "direction, supervision, or control" over curriculum, instruction, materials selection, or hiring (Public Law 89–10, Section 604, 1965), states' fears of federal control persist. Although not directly involved in the writing of the CCS, the federal government made four policy moves to incentivize states to adopt them. In the same speech to the NGA quoted at the beginning of this section, President Obama announced that he would like to make federal Title 1 funding contingent on states adopting the standards (Klein, 2010). In the regulations for Race to the Top, states that adopted the CCS by August 2, 2010, would be awarded extra points in the competition for a portion of the $4.5 billion in federal innovation funding (Lewin, 2010). In exchange for agreeing to adopt the CCS and test-based teacher evaluation, Secretary of Education Arne Duncan granted states waivers from adequate yearly progress quotas set under the No Child Left Behind (NCLB) law, saving many schools from being categorized as "failing" (Perez-Pena, 2012). As Gates mentioned in the previous quote, President Obama provided $350 million to two agencies (Smarter Balanced Assessment Consortium and Partnership for Assessment of Readiness for College and Career) to develop break-the-mold Common Core assessments. Forty-six states and the District of Columbia accepted the standards.

During the fall of 2013, CCS straddled the tensions within schooling for economic development, equality of opportunity, and global standing. Advocates explained that CCS will meliorate the tensions soon, and they worked strategically to complete the positioning of students for success (Obama) by aligning standards with curricula and assessments (Gates). They worried, however, because the 46 states that adopted the CCS had yet to complete their production or purchase of common curricula, the adoption of common assessments, or the negotiation of common passing scores. Despite the rhetoric that full implementation would take place in 2014, CCS was still open to interpretation and the alignment project was still being negotiated. Ten state legislatures considered bills to drop out of the Common Core agreement altogether or to withhold its implementation until there was empirical evidence of the superiority of the common standards and assessments over state standards and assessments in the production of graduates who are college and career ready and able to compete in the global innovation economy.

In the Brown Center Report on American Education, Tom Loveless (2012) argued that it's unlikely that evidence of superiority will be easily found. Common standards cannot be the sole cause of high scores on international tests, he cautioned, because countries scoring above and below the United States have common standards. Even alignment of the standards, tests, and curriculum cannot fully account for high scores because Finland and New Zealand produce high scores but deemphasize testing (Sahlberg, 2011). Moreover, despite common standards *within* each state, achievement gaps persisted among demographic groups. Although the racial achievement gap narrowed slightly during NCLB, the income achievement gap actually widened during that time. If uniformity of standards (a common core) was the solution, then the gap within states should have narrowed markedly over the last decade. It did not.

According to Loveless, the quality of the standards and the rigor with which they are implemented does not have a strong record either. Citing Whitehurst (2009), Loveless found that neither the quality of state standards as judged by experts nor high state cutoff scores for proficiency predicted student achievement because, "within-state variation is four or five times larger than the variation between states" (p. 4). He adopted a popular (but not flattering) CCS metaphor to explain this statistical finding. While advocates claim that CCS will overcome the achievement differences between students in Massachusetts (more rigor) and Mississippi (less rigor), Loveless showed that each state already had mini-Massachusetts and mini-Mississippi contrasts within its borders. Loveless admitted that skeptics might be justified in questioning the wisdom and expense of CCS.

Hess (2010) warns against such instrumental thinking. Requiring innovators to prove the outcome of their enterprise before attempting change overestimates the power of science, fears change, and misunderstands the role of markets. Insisting on small-scale studies that demonstrate short-term outcomes, while potentially useful, has also led historically to waves of ill-fated reforms in American schools—open architecture, new math, and mastery learning to name a few—because the reasoning behind them was flawed. Requests for certainty of outcome before initiating change assumes that the status quo is tenable; however, state-controlled traditional schools cannot address the challenges posed in the global innovation economy. School change is necessary if America is to compete. Finally, those who seek validation before initiatives begin to neglect the dynamic importance of competition and the market's ability to direct resources efficiently to the options for which there is the most demand. As Gates explained, the national scope of CCS is essential to begin this process that will eventually produce more ecosystems of empowered people able to invent the future.

Neoliberals understand poverty as the lack of human capital sufficient to gain and maintain a sustainable income for oneself and one's family during rapidly changing times. Poverty stems from two sources. Poor individuals do not possess a realistic understanding of the demands placed on workers within the world in which we are living and, therefore, do not develop the requisite entrepreneurial disposition to continuously adapt to changes. Consequently, they do not demand institutional changes that will position them to prosper within the global competitions. In turn, government officials have not developed the physical and human infrastructure appropriately to increase the productive capacities of individuals, regions, and the nation in order to meet and beat the competitors around the world. Government inaction, or misguided action toward equity or cultural issues, handicaps the economy, crippling its competitiveness and threatening lower- and middle-income individuals with the inevitability of poverty. Neoliberals argue that this is the current state of American society, and in order to address poverty, Americans must change their priorities and insist that government officials develop conditions in which flexible institutions can use market forces to anticipate, create, and deliver "more high value-added service and manufactured goods" (Friedman, 2012).

Reading education plays a prominent role in realizing the neoliberal solution to poverty; however, its form, teacher dispositions, and school curriculum must change. All American children and youth must reach a minimum proficiency with reading complex texts in order to attract a sustaining wage from employers across their lifespan, and they must recognize that they are in a struggle for their economic well-being from early childhood. Common core standards enhanced with the four Cs, smart tool literacy, and interdisciplinary themes of global awareness, finance, civics, health matters, and environmental issues will produce school graduates who are college or career ready at a globally competitive level. Because 100 years of scientific experimentation has yet to identify the one best method of teaching all students to read proficiently, reading education must be unbundled from schooling-as-we-know-it in order to "unleash a powerful market of people providing services for better teaching" (Gates, 2009). Neoliberals point to New Orleans, KIPP, and YES Prep as examples of how unbundling and competition can provide better teaching services for the niche market of poor and low-income students. Such examples might seem paternalistic as Neuman and Celano (2012) charge, but they attract capital from governments, foundations, and corporations and prepare students to adapt to the world in which we are living. As CCS architect David Coleman explained during a presentation to the New York State Department of Education in April 2011:

> The fifth point is about writing. Do people know the two most popular forms of writing in the American high school today? Texting someone said: I don't think that's for credit though yet. But I would say that as some said it is personal writing. It is either the exposition of a personal opinion or it is the presentation of a personal matter. The only problem, forgive me for saying this so bluntly, the only problem with those two forms of writing is as you grow up in this world you realize people don't give a shit about what you feel or what you think. What they instead care about is can you make an argument with evidence, is there something verifiable behind what you're saying or what you think or feel that you can demonstrate to me. It is rare in a working environment that someone says, "Johnson, I need a market analysis by Friday, but before that I need a compelling account of your childhood." That is rare. (Coleman, 2011)

6
COLLECTIVE AGENCY
Radical Democrats

"Mikey Dillion, you're rich!"
"Take it easy."
"You are. You're terrific."
"I'm not rich."
"Oh, what do you call it?"
"I don't know."
"W-e-a-l-thy?"
"No, just comfortable."
"You're comfortable. Okay, I guess that makes me *un-*comfortable. Is that what you call us low-ly people? Un-comfortable?"
"No."
"I like that; it's nicer than rich. And you *look* comfortable."
"Funny, I don't feel comfortable in this conversation."

These lines are from David Lindsay-Abaire's (2012) *Good People,* the most-produced play in the United States during the 2012 theater season. The brief exchange takes place in Act II at Mike Dillion's house in Chestnut Hill, a wealthy Boston suburb. His inquisitor is Margaret Walsh, his brief high school sweetheart, who took the train from South Boston to his home prepared to capitalize on their former relationship by asking his birthday party guests for a job. After 30 years apart, she needs Mike's help because she has just been fired from her job at the Dollar Store, is about to become behind on her rent, and has an adult intellectually dependent daughter at home born eight months after their relationship ended. Desperate for a favor, but unable to code switch, Margie taunts Mike about his good luck and good fortune, expecting him to recognize comradely sniping and respond with Southie loyalty. *Good People* has much to say about the economy and how it works for and against different classes of Americans.

During interviews, Lindsay-Abaire explained that while the plot is fictional, he based the narrative on his personal experience. He was born in South Boston, a working-class neighborhood, the son of a fruit seller from a truck at the Chelsea Market (father) and factory worker (mother). When he was 12, the leaders at his neighborhood Boys and Girls Club negotiated a scholarship for him to attend Milton Academy, a prestigious suburban boarding school. After graduation, he attended Sarah Lawrence College and Julliard on fellowships. His plays have won many awards—a Pulitzer Prize, Drama Circle Award, and Kisselring Prize. Lindsay-Abaire acknowledged: "I wasn't interested in writing any didactic, message laden play . . . [but] if I write about Southie in any way, class will inevitably bubble up to the surface" (as quoted in Adams, 2012). Like all text, *Good People* is open to interpretation. Take, for example, the following quotes.

> Margie's reason for looking up Mike is an all too familiar one in the current economy. . . . The social dichotomy being explored isn't a matter of black and white. It's who does and doesn't escape from where he or she comes from . . . there's nothing pure about the goodness or badness of the folks who inhabit this play. (Ben Brantley, *New York Times*, March 3, 2011)

> In Mr. Lindsay-Abaire's America, success is *purely* a matter of luck, and virtue inheres solely in those who are luckless. So what if Mikey worked hard? Why should anybody deserve any credit for working hard? Hence the crude deck-stacking built into the script of "Good People" in which Mikey is the callous villain who forgot where he came from and Margie the plucky Southie gal who may be the least little bit racist, but is otherwise a perfect heroine victim. (Terry Teachout, *Wall Street Journal*, March 4, 2011)

> *Good People* is a meditation on class, social mobility, and the viability of the American Dream. . . . But the play is far from parochial. Its broader theme, especially timely in an election year, is part of an anxious national conversation about the tattered American dream of opportunity, hard work, and meritocracy. (Prospero, *The Economist*, October 10, 2012)

> What struck me, after the standing ovation and on the drive home, was that the play's working class characters, surrounded by all the social ills of poverty, never once ask why the world they live in is the way it is. No one in the play has any perspective on their condition or what keeps them there. In Lindsay-Abaire's play, the poor have been beaten into submission and the "comfortable" are unwilling to rock the boat for fear of falling back in to the icy sea. No one even considers rebellion as an option. (Richard Adams, *The World Socialist Web Site*, April 18, 2012)

These critics provide a literacy lesson that many liberals, conservatives, and neoliberals neglect in their visions of reading education. The critics recognize that playwright Lindsay-Abaire engages in public pedagogy to teach his audience what they should know, who they should be, and what they should value about social class in America. Many theaters across the United States produced the play to teach lessons as well. The critics interpret the playwright's symbols that he embedded subtly in his play in order to create their meaning and evaluate its intended lessons. To be sure, Lindsay-Abaire's symbols are reinterpreted through the many professionals involved in the play's productions and performances, and the critics attend to the craft and art of each, commenting on the set, costumes, lighting, and staging as well as the look, sound, and movement of the actors. However, the thrust of those comments was concerned with how these reinterpretations enhance or detract from the meaning they ultimately make from Lindsay-Abaire's play. In this case, the critics acknowledge explicitly that the public pedagogy of *Good People* is part of larger ideological struggles to position the audience and capture their allegiance concerning class in America. And they lavish praise and find fault according to their positions within these ideological struggles. Their exchange is not just a discussion of aesthetics; rather, it's an argument over whose vision best fits the current social circumstances.

In this way, *Good People* and its critics demonstrate that writing and reading are recursive political acts vital within a democracy. Lindsay-Abaire rereads his experience and those of others from South Boston and rewrites them through the symbols he chooses to represent his meaning. Although he hoped his symbolism wasn't didactic, he admits that he intended to teach about class in America in order to represent and frame poverty for audiences. During the performances they viewed, the critics attend to those symbols according to their ideological understandings of class, and then, in turn, they engage in the public pedagogy of theater criticism by placing their reviews in specific publications with established readerships. Think about *New York Times* critic Brantley's liberal characterization of opportunities to escape poverty. Note *Wall Street Journal* critic Teachout's conservative class warfare salvo about character and choice. Prospero touches on liberal opportunity and conservative hard work before closing with neoliberal competition/rewards based on merit. Socialist Adams laments the absence of social realism in *Good People* without an option of rebellion among the masses. The critics and Lindsay-Abaire engage in an agonistic battle concerning whose "story" about class should be believed (Mouffe, 2007). Reading and writing are certainly tools with which all participants are able to make a living, as liberal, conservatives, and neoliberals acknowledge, but they are also clearly weapons they use in ideological struggles to teach audiences about themselves and others. The latter is a fundamental concept in radical democratic reading education.

In this chapter I read *Good People* in order to demonstrate how its symbols portray a radical democratic position on poverty and to establish the need for economically, culturally, and politically explicit forms of reading education to equip the poor with the tools and weapons to participate more fully in the decisions that affect their lives. Radical Democrats disrupt liberal, conservative, and neoliberal representations and frames of reading education because they provide neither the theories nor the practices necessary to fill that need. Under a variety of labels, however, educators offer examples of theories and practices of reading education that fit within radical democratic principles and offer a different vision of the future for the poor. Some developed countries with lower rates of child poverty and higher reading test scores have officially recognized these needs and invite radical democratic theories and practices into school classrooms. I close the book with a hypothesis and an argument that radical democratic visions of poverty and reading education best fit the needs of most Americans.

A Radical Democratic View of Poverty

In the short dialogue quoted at the start of the chapter, Margie and Mike present the essence of democracy in which different groups express their disparate interests in deciding how we should live together. Margie seeks a modicum of *redistribution* of income through employment at a wage that could provide adequately for herself and her daughter. Her appeal requires Mike to acknowledge two forms of *recognition*—that they were/are both Southies and that she is now living among "lowly people," who provide the products and services that enable him to be comfortable. Mike deflects Margie's characterization of their current economic and cultural situations, implying that while they might differ they could live harmoniously as good Americans. Just her mention of modest redistribution and recognition makes him uncomfortable. Yet, the power differential between the two is clear throughout these few lines because the "lowly" might snipe, but they will be denied *representation* in the final decisions. From a radical democratic vantage point (Fraser, 2009), *Good People* represents poverty as having economic, cultural, and political dimensions in contemporary America. It frames poverty as injustice and it promises action toward *justice through participatory parity*.

Redistribution

During the play, Margie lacks income because she works at the neighborhood Dollar Store that pays her $9.20 an hour. If she works 40 hours each week for a year, then she and her daughter are a low-income family—$3,000 above the poverty line. If her work week falls to 30 hours, then they live in poverty. In the opening scene the store manager, Steve, explains to Margie that the central office ordered all managers to enforce the time-card regulations or be fired. Margie's time card records that she has been late often and, therefore, must be "let go." Margie reminds Steve that she is late because her daughter's care provider does not arrive on time, and her daughter, although a 30-year-old adult, can't be left alone. On her retail wages, she explains, she has no other options but to wait for her sitter. Other good people straddle the low-income line as well. Jean, Margie's friend, lacks income because the caterer she works for doesn't offer enough work hours or any benefits. Widower Dottie, Margie's landlord and her daughter's care provider, relies on Margie's rent and the sale of simple crafts (that Margie's daughter makes for her during the day). Dottie's son is now desperate because his job disappeared, along with the company he worked for, and his wife's hours were cut back. If Margie can't pay the rent on time, Dottie repeatedly cautions, she'll be forced to move her son into the flat. Margie's employment possibilities are limited because her car was repossessed after she broke a tooth and "chose" to pay the dentist instead of the bank.

Mike and Kate, his wife, are comfortable because his reproductive endocrinology practice thrives and her literature classes at Boston University are well enrolled. They have developed their human capital to fit the changing times while Margie and the others have not. Mike tells Margie he is unable to offer her a job at his office because she doesn't have the proper skills, the receptionist position is filled, and cleaning services are subcontracted. When Kate offered Margie a position watching their son in Mike's home, Kate apologized because they would only pay $15 per hour. Margie is eager for the two-thirds bump in her income, but Mike objects that Margie's disposition is not right for that position either. This rejection sets off a firestorm of cultural accusations.

Recognition

Recognition is complicated in *Good People*—characters clash over the legitimacy of cultural values among different groups. In the opening scene in which Steve fires Margie, she equivocates between appeals to her friendship with Steve's mother and derogatory accusations about his sexuality (he plays bingo two nights a week) and his favoritism of a younger Asian employee (who makes less per hour). Margie acknowledges the common plight among Jean, Dottie, and herself, smoothing Jean's sharp quips about Dottie's exploitation of Margie and her daughter with statements about her continued support as well. Given the racial tensions in the South Boston of their youth, Margie is surprised that Mike's receptionist is an immigrant from the Dominican Republic and Kate is African American. Critics Teachout and Brantley both mention recognition of race in their reviews. Teachout comments on Margie's apparent racism and Brantley argues that opportunity, not racism, is the stumbling block for social mobility.

After mistaking Margie for the party's catering help, Kate recognizes the sisterhood among women in trouble. She invites Margie to stay, although the party has been cancelled due to her son's illness, and probes her about Mike's early years. Kate wants to know about South Boston's mean streets that Mike escaped. Kate is, however, less inclined to recognize her racial similarities to Mike's receptionist because she has recently uncovered Mike's affair with her. Kate's compassion for single-mother Margie wanes when Kate learns that Mike and Margie were lovers

30 years ago and that a baby followed Mike's departure for college. Critic Adams bristled at Kate's choice of comfort over solidarity and her insistence that Margie deny that her daughter is actually Mike's child.

Mike seeks to be recognized as a Southie who made it and as justified in his right to be comfortable. Since their marriage, he has romanticized his youth to Kate, claiming street credibility while demonstrating his control of codes of "comfort" through acquisition and consumption. Mike appears to be colorblind regarding his wife and receptionist, but Margie reports that what enabled Mike to leave South Boston was that his father stopped Mike and others from beating a Black youth to death because he strayed beyond his territory. If someone hadn't been looking out for him, she concludes, Mike would have left South Boston for Walpole Prison instead of college. Although both Margie and he had worked hard since that time, Mike's hard work counted more because it took place outside of Southie.

Lindsay-Abaire's theme of Mike's sexual relationships throughout the play can't be by chance. Mike "screwed" lowly Margie, his third-world receptionist, and acceptable African American Kate—and now sells fertility to the comfortable—in order to make it. This must be a symbol of exploitation in America. When Margie cries that she didn't tell Mike about her pregnancy because he was headed to college, Mike replies "it wouldn't have mattered." He was gone regardless. Beyond his receptionist, Kate reports that Mike has had many affairs since their wedding, and that they are working on their marriage (although Mike resents her need for couple's counseling). In Mike's case, recognition of class, race, and gender differences is portrayed as an externality to his ambition in a highly competitive society, and then, it appears to be his reward for his hard work. Mike believes that he's not responsible for the unforeseen consequences of his actions—after all, he is good people.

Representation

Representation is primarily asymmetrical in *Good People*. Hierarchies are apparent and enforced throughout the play. Mike decides to attend college and pregnant Margie has a daughter alone. Dollar Store management decides time cards matter, Steve complies, and Margie has no choice but to accept. The caterers decide part-time employment suits their business model, and Jean and others become underemployed. At home, Dottie decides the rent is due, and Margie frets. Mike's receptionist decides no meeting without an appointment, and Margie comes another time. Mike decides on Margie's employment as their caregiver, and Kate and Margie move on. In all instances, decision rules empower some and deny others in the process of deliberation regardless of the human relations involved or the likely consequences for people not represented in the decision making. Critic Adams describes this as the poor being beaten into submission and the "comfortable's" fear of falling down the chutes camouflaged along the class boundaries. He identifies little agency and concludes: "No one in the play has any perspective on their condition or what keeps them there."

I do find it curious that government is not mentioned in *Good People*. There are liberal laws established to protect the rights of injured parties in hierarchical power relationships and to support those in need. Although Margie works many angles when Steve fires her, she never threatens a wrongful termination suit. No one mentions laws regarding sexual harassment in the workplace, a paternity suit, or divorce, although each could alter power relations and leverage more authority for the less powerful within certain decisions. Although Margie would not be eligible for unemployment insurance because she was fired for cause, Jean and Dottie never consider it a possibility when they try to think of alternative ways for Margie to sustain herself and her daughter. Temporary Assistance to Needy Families, Section 8 of Low Income Housing Assistance, Supplemental Nutrition Assistance Program (SNAP), Medicaid, and Supplemental Security Income could aid Margie in her time of need, but they are never considered in *Good People*. It must be that Lindsay-Abaire sees the government as complicit in maintaining the status quo.

Justice Through Participatory Parity

At the end of the play, Margie, Jean, Dottie, and Steve sit side-by-side at a bingo table discussing Margie's options. Something has changed, however. Dottie has just received an anonymous envelope filled with cash for Margie's rent. Jean is sure that Mike has sent it as a form of apology, and perhaps, as a sign that he accepts some responsibility for the family's predicament. While Jean and Dottie wonder what Mike's next move might be, Margie will have none of it—she asks Dottie to send the money back because she wants nothing to do with Mike. With that possibility, Steve confesses that he paid Margie's rent with his bingo winnings from the week before. After a moment's pause, Margie grasps Steve's hand, thanks him, calls the gesture a loan, and vows to pay it back. Steve says that he's sure that she will as Jean and Dottie nod in recognition. They smile at each other in solidarity, lowering their heads for a moment to record the bingo caller's coordinates, and then simultaneously, they look up at the audience.

Among the critics, the last scene troubles Adams because the characters don't explicitly discuss "why the world they live in is the way it is." Brantley notes a "feisty defeatism" among the Southies. And, Teachout writes, "the play's bait-and-switch semi-happy ending . . . negates all that has come before it." The critics doubt that the poor are competent enough to decide their own futures. This last point is an important difference between radical democratic and liberal, conservative, and neoliberal concepts of the poor.

Liberals view the differences between the lowly and the comfortable as deficits that must be systematically repaired by experts using the best practices that will enable the poor to contribute to society effectively.

Conservatives doubt the capacities of the poor to make good choices for themselves, and, therefore, they encourage the poor to adopt good character traits and appropriate knowledge before they might be permitted to participate more fully in the social order.

Neoliberals understand the poor as losers in life's competitions. They are, therefore, unlikely to invent a viable social future for themselves or others. At best, they can become consumers, and at worst, they become a social expense. In order to avoid the latter, the poor must acquire sufficient human capital to attract sustainable wages.

Despite their obvious differences, liberals, conservatives, and neoliberals insist that the poor conform to accepted academic, moral, and market standards in order to earn the right to think, plan, and act in society.

From a radical democratic perspective, however, there is a much more hopeful promise for the future in the last scene of *Good People*. Despite the best public pedagogical attempts of business and the rich to teach their common-sense views of the social order—keeping the four feeling personally responsible for their economic circumstances, denying the legitimacy of their cultural values, and excluding them from decisions that affect their lives—Margie, Jean, Dottie, and Steve make several radical democratic moves. First, after witnessing Margie's struggles, they use their sociological imaginations to see that poverty is not her personal trouble but, rather, their shared social issue (Mills, 1959). Rather than despair, this causes a shift among their diverse identities, prioritizing their economic interests over the other interests they have (Mouffe, 2009). They become aware that if they are to survive the world in which they are living, they must find ways to work together in order to name issues that befall them and to address them accordingly (Fraser, 2009). To be sure, they will seek more income, but they'll also work to be recognized as cultural beings—more than just their exchange values—as they claim just representation in decision making about the quality of their lives. When they gaze at the audience together in that final moment, they seem to be wondering if they have allies among the crowd—as if to ask, "what are you good people going to do with these lessons from our lives?" With that action, they begin to lead rather than follow.

Radical Democratic Solutions to Poverty

In the public spaces of the theater, and then, in the newspapers, magazines, and websites of theater criticism, Lindsay-Abaire and the critics challenge and/or maintain the symbolic order of poverty in American life. From a radical democratic viewpoint, Lindsay-Abaire unveils what is repressed in the common consensus about the rich and the poor. The government is not an impartial provider of opportunities for all (liberal). No group has a monopoly on virtue because all characters played the roles of "good" people (conservative). The invisible hand of the market metaphor—everyone looking out for him- or herself through rational self-interest—does not lead to the well-being of society (neoliberal). Without a heavy hand, the playwright makes visible the oppression, the continuous stress, and hardships of the poor behind that consensus. Multiple factors contribute to Margie's present condition—lack of child care, goods available only through "bargain" retailers, access to transportation, adequate health care, and fund raising/jackpot recreation. She finds herself, and they find themselves, in a nexus of economic, social, cultural, political, and ecological relations that have no single identifiable cause. Rather, their poverty is overdetermined (Yapa, 1996). A good job would help Margie, but it is not the only factor influencing the quality of her life.

Moreover, the play's ending suggests that the poor have become the subjects who study, rather than the objects of study. Through their actions, talk, and eventual coalition, Margie, Dottie, Jean, and Steve reject the liberal, conservative, and neoliberal constructs of the poor as deficient, lazy, or losers and begin to construct new identities for the poor as collective agents of change (Yapa, 1996). They question the norms of the consensus position concerning the poor and poverty. They analyze the empirical data they gather during those inquiries and compare them against their own experiences. They draw conclusions based on those analyses, and then choose a course of action. Although their plan does not end their poverty, to be sure, it sets up conditions under which issues of redistribution, recognition, and representation could be addressed effectively through the new community network that has just emerged in the public space of the bingo hall. This collective agency does not absolve business, government, the rich, or poverty experts of responsibility; however, it locates the power to name, learn, plan, and work within the hands of the poor. Their gaze, then, is not a search for salvation, but an effort to expand their network of expertise to help address their priorities among challenges they face.

And challenges await. By representing poverty as multidimensional with specific instantiations for diverse groups in specific locations, radical democrats open multiple sites and ways in which substantive actions can be initiated. This representation places the poor as the ones who know the most about their poverty—not necessarily in the abstract academic discursive sense, but in the material, physiological, and spiritual senses of daily experience. Yet, the individuals positioned as the poor have other identities as well, complete with other interests, and perhaps, competing priorities. Moreover, as well dramatized in *Good People,* the groups have been positioned to be in direct competition with one another around issues of sexuality, age, race, and gender. The collective nature of the poor's agency, then, must be understood as hard won, temporary, and precious. Multiple collectives are possible within one community based on poor + other identity coalitions, addressing several specific substantive issues simultaneously. The plurality of interests, goals, and actions should keep the community reflexive against the possibilities of new consensus about poverty forming around new types of exclusions. Framing poverty as injustice, while seeking justice through participatory parity, means that the poor's articulations of issues, coalitions, and actions will be continuously developing, contracting, and expanding.

Over the past 80 years, The Highlander Research and Education Center (formerly the Highlander Folk School) engaged in developing collective agency among community groups in Appalachia and the south in order to promote social, racial, and economic justice. It's most famous founder and director, Myles Horton, had studied the positive possibilities of social conflict with Robert Park and education-as-action with Lester Ward, and after visiting Danish Folk Schools concluded that the solutions to social problems could be found in the collective intelligence and social action of a community, once the community members believed themselves capable masters of their own fate. Early workshops for labor unions (as the de facto CIO education center) and civil rights groups (Montgomery bus boycott, citizenship schools, and Student Nonviolent Coordinating Committee) were followed by work on ecological, globalization, and immigration concerns. According to Horton, leaders sought to elicit and develop community members' capacities to learn—how to analyze problems, sharpen questions, recognize connections, draw conclusions, and test the new knowledge when community members returned home.

> In a real sense, they bring not only their subject with them, but they bring their curriculum. That curriculum is their experience. We do what, I guess, you would think of as peer learning. We think the best teachers of poor people are the poor people themselves. The best teachers about Black problems are the Black people. The best teachers about Appalachian problems are Appalachians and so on. We're there to help them do what they want and come to their own conclusions. (Myles Horton, April 1975, as quoted in Dropkin & Tobier, 1975, p. 75)

In his January 18, 2013, blog post, "This Week in Poverty," Greg Kaufman (2013) identifies "the anti-poverty movement—and I do believe it's a movement," a swelling of community groups working on income, housing, health care, and hunger issues across the United States. Consider his take on the radical democratic Witnesses to Hunger programs that began in Philadelphia, a city with 28 percent of its citizens living below the poverty line and 200,000 living in deep poverty. In order to inform others about poverty, Witnesses take photographs that represent their lives and speak about the priorities in their communities. They formed information groups in their neighborhoods for support and direction. Exhibitions have been given nationally and the Witnesses have testified to local, state, and national officials. Witnesses programs have emerged in Boston, Providence, and Baltimore with prospects in many other cities. Their work has been credited in Philadelphia's 2013 Shared Prosperity program, which placed access to all state and federal antipoverty services in one location within North Philadelphia and employed client advocates to ensure services to those who are eligible.

Good People, the Highlander Research and Education Center, and Witnesses to Hunger provide examples of ongoing literate social practices among the poor. In a variety of circumstances and toward various ends, adults question economic, cultural, and political norms; collect data and analyze them, comparing them to their experience; make connections; and draw conclusions and act discursively and physically as collective agents to improve the quality of their lives. To be sure, these practices are partial and developing continuously through interactions with others across time and place. Glynda Hull and Elizabeth Moje (2012) connect such social practices to the lives of youth and children, suggesting that students bring these home and community-based reading practices with them to school at differing levels of facility and with differing types of symbols. Like the Highlander educators in the search for reflexive justice (Fraser, 2009), radical democratic teachers can help students sharpen, deepen, and extend their literate practices to name, learn, plan, and work toward redistribution, recognition, and representation in their daily lives.

Radical Democratic Reading Education

From a radical democratic standpoint, everything is text. That is, everything is social, touched by human choices and actions. Nothing built, private, or natural should escape our reading because it was influenced by the social and is designed to influence others. Think of the various ways people represent water as public, private, natural, free, bottled, frozen, fresh, polluted, recreation, life. These representations are offered through different media, modalities, and symbol systems, and they are framed according to the authors' ideologies that are often not readily apparent. Consider private swimming pools in desert areas, homes without running water or melting ice caps. People must read these things/texts accurately in order to gain social competence while negotiating their daily lives and to connect their lives to those of others by imagining likely and possible consequences. If radical democrats seek reflexive justice through participatory parity, then readers must "refrain from jumping too quickly to conclusions shaped by what we once believed to be true and good" (Lemert, 2008, p. x).

In many cases, past consensus about what were considered normal choices, dispositions, and actions did not serve all social groups well or justly. Radical democrats point to many historical and contemporary examples in which consensus has been used as a tool and a weapon to protect privileged groups. Reading with social competence within such environments invites readers to conform, even when many social texts around them are inhospitable, even hostile. Reading to fit into hostile environments might be tactical; however, as radical democrats argue, it is neither just nor democratic. Rather, radical democrats seek reading with sociological imagination to question past consensus, to see the dynamic powers of difference, and to act on their new knowledge.

Preschool

In *Negotiating Critical Literacies with Young Children* Vivian Vasquez (2004) describes vividly a radical democratic reading curriculum developed with three- and four-year-old students in a Toronto junior kindergarten classroom. Her students came from diverse cultural and linguistic backgrounds with nearly half being recent immigrants. From the children's conversations and questions during the first week of school, Vasquez concluded that they possessed sufficient language and curiosity to pursue in depth some of the questions they raised about their lives. She imagined negotiation and contestation at the center of this curriculum as students and she adjusted and reconstructed what they knew about the world in order to have some impact on that world. Across the academic year during their two and half hours a day together, they asked questions, gathered data, discussed and analyzed them, described what they found, located themselves within the findings, and took action. To help them move from oral to written language, they kept an image and print audit trail of artifacts they collected or made, carefully recording their social theories on a bulletin board. Vasquez does not propose the curriculum or pedagogy as a model for others, but rather offers it as a set of possibilities of what preschool students did and can do when their teachers take them and critical reading seriously.

Junior kindergarten is part of the province's tax-supported public schooling with a mandated curriculum. In order to develop the curriculum from students' questions and interests, Vasquez had to demonstrate how their work together met, if not surpassed, those standards. For example, a reading standard required teachers to "use a variety of materials for information and pleasure." Engagements in the negotiated curriculum included pictures, magazines, newspapers, flyers, encyclopedias, websites, cultural texts from children's homes, and songs. The curriculum mandates told teachers to "write simple messages." Together and separately Vasquez's students wrote letters, surveys, posters, petitions, lists, newsletters, songs, stories, poems, instruction sheets, warnings, agendas, and conference programs. To negotiate the space for this curriculum, Vasquez maintained open and frequent contact with her colleagues, supervisors, and the children's parents. In school, this meant asking for and providing help to other junior kindergarten and kindergarten teachers pursuing different curricula and speaking candidly with administrators about her struggles, missteps, and triumphs and inviting them into the classroom. With parents, Vasquez asked for ideas and help in order to explore cultural differences and representations. These negotiations extended and led to compromise, but never moved Vasquez and her students away from their frame of reading as social critique, social analysis, and social action.

Across the academic year, Vasquez and the students inquired about ecology (rainforests), access (the school's language program), recognition (vegetarians and food service), and pollution (St. Lawrence River and Lake Ontario). All topics arose from conversations among the students and became significant because the conversations continued over days. During the spring, students began a conversation about the toys in McDonald's Happy Meals that developed into discussions of gender, consumerism, desire, and social connections. Girls complained that they were given Barbies instead of the Hot Wheels unless they asked specifically for a switch to be made. Students recognized that toys changed periodically because: "Well, if they didn't change the toys I wouldn't go" (Vasquez, 2004, p. 125). Students understood that McDonald's labeling of the toys as collectables and introducing them in a series over time produced desire among children to frequent the restaurant regularly, even if "they have seven kids in their family" (Vasquez, 2004, p. 127). McDonald's advertised the toys as free, but "the price of the toy is in the bag" (Vasquez, 2004, p. 129). At the beginning of the inquiry, students were able to supply five components of a Happy Meal—hamburger, toy, fries, drink, and bag. By the end of the study, they had made over 50 explicit connections, commenting on steel work for the fry basket to ad designers for cups and signs to farmers for meat and vegetables and the gas company for cooking. During their theorizing, they concluded, "actually that tells me McDonald's knows how we think. But now. Now, we know how they think. Aha!" (Vasquez, 2004, p. 125).

The last text Vasquez and her students produced together was a list of what next year's junior kindergarteners should know. Among the statements were:

> Listen to other kids;
> If there's something happening in the school and you want to go, you can make something like a petition; and
> You can be strong from your brain. (Vasquez, 2004, p. 26)

Elementary

Timothy O'Keefe teaches second- and third-grade students at the Center for Inquiry in greater Columbia, South Carolina. The Center is a magnet school (with a lottery to determine enrollment) based on the notion that "students, parents and staff . . . are responsible for developing ourselves as more thoughtful, caring, and intelligent people who delight in learning and are committed to creating a more compassionate, equitable, knowledgeable and democratic world" (website mission statement). One path toward that goal is the use of literature "to help children live beyond their ordinary lives—to come to understand, from the inside, about other people, other places, and other times" (Mills, Stephens, & O'Keefe, 2004, p. 49). True to its name, the teachers at the Center take the stance that reading literature is an inquiry; as a fifth grader commented: "Oh, so now I'm beginning to see that reading is like having a conversation with the author" (Mills et al., 2004, p. 50). Those conversations are treated as personal, with individuals mixing the author's points with their past experiences, as well as social, when students come together to talk about the meanings that they've made. The challenge for teachers within that dialectic is not to force consensus among the readers around a particular meaning or position, but to appreciate the possibilities of dissensus—"collective explanations of how people differ, where their differences come from, and whether they can live and work together with these differences" (Trimbur, 1992, p. 216).

The Center for Inquiry is a public school and, therefore, must comply with South Carolina's interpretations of No Child Left Behind, Race to the Top, and Common Core Standards. In order to make space for their commitments, teachers meet once a week to study themselves through "curricular conversations" (Mills, Jennings, Donnelly, & Mueller, 2001). During these meetings, teachers acknowledge the challenges that emerge when curriculum revolves around students' understandings and their willingness to negotiate those understandings publicly. In this forum, teachers take up issues of authority, bias, and misconceptions and consider classroom artifacts and recordings of lessons. Individual talents and interests direct teachers to discover and develop different ways in which to pursue the Center's commitments.

For example, O'Keefe shared a transcript of a small group discussion of Lois Lowry's short story, *The Tree House* (Mills et al., 2004). The story is about two neighbor children who conflict over access to an elegant tree house that a grandfather built as a present. Hurt by the exclusion, the neighbor retaliates with a tree house of her own built with available scraps of lumber. The conflict escalates to antagonism around the neighbors' rhetoric of ownership and pride, and then breaks when loneliness overtakes first one and then the other neighbor. O'Keefe uses the transcript to track students' worries ("If she whispered it, how could Chrissy hear her?"), feelings ("Just to brag"), and interpretations ("I wrote that didn't mean anything"). They tackle what keeps people apart: private property ("Her grandpa said that it was just for her"), stereotypes ("The guy made Chrissy think that Leah was bad"), and fences ("She means the fence is above your height"). And they discuss what brings people together—bridges ("And then they could walk across") and understanding ("If we each came out half way and held hands we could help each other across"). After the discussions, O'Keefe and the group listen to recordings in order to reflect on the parity among participants and the recognition and representation among members. Beyond the reading of printed texts, they also learn to read others, themselves, and possible uses for literature in their lives.

> Reading can do lots of things. It can make you smart; it can make you love people. Without reading, the world would be different. . . . Reading is power. (third-grade student as quoted in Mills et al., 2004, p. 47)

High School

In *Harlem on Our Minds,* Valerie Kinloch (2009) presents a negative print of current urban school reform, describing what schools are and showing what they could become. Typical schooling takes students out of their communities, marginalizes their knowledge, and assumes disinterest. By following two male adolescents during a year-long English class, Kinloch displays that schooling could be project-oriented, authentic, and deeply engaging. Although the state testing systems direct high school students toward facts from British and American literature, formulaic writing, and individual mastery, the teacher's pedagogies and students' engagements demonstrate that learning is contextual, meaning oriented, and collaborative. The official curriculum treats reading as singular, print-based, and complete. Phillip and Khaleeq, two high school student participants of Kinloch's study, show that reading is multiple, multimodal, and continuous. Kinloch (2009) admits the experience changed her definition of literacy "from a quite narrow to a much more expansive conception: as acts of, practices in, and activities around reading, writing, speaking . . .[and] a variety of media" (pp. 8–9).

Kinloch's report begins in Latoya Hartman's mixed-level English class (some students had already passed the state English exam required for graduation). After students read and discussed works of Assata Shalur, June Jordan, Elie Wiesel, and Frederick Douglas, Hartman asked: "How would you respond to the dilemmas raised in these books in your local community?" (Kinloch, 2009, p. 26). The question prompted Phillip and Khaleeq to address the ongoing process of gentrification in their neighborhood and its physical, social, and psychological effects on their neighbors. They stretched their academic literacies in order to consider historical and contemporary representations of gentrification in Harlem, encountering multiple ideological frames as they conducted interviews about their neighborhood with its residents. In order to demonstrate their inventory of past and present community resources, they moved out of the classroom and into their community, relying on their developing control of print, photography and video, sound recording, and even movement. During the inquiry, Hartman and Kinloch intervened in Phillip's and Khaleeq's work to push on their too-quick certainties, to support and extend their uses of language, and to provide multiple forums for them to present their work to different audiences.

To her credit, Kinloch tells complicated, overdetermined stories about gentrification, place, and reading. Within the process of gentrification, clearly one type of community is valued over another; however, Kinloch represents multiple perspectives among the community members by giving them space to write their stories within her book. These voices harmonize at times, but are discordant at others, demonstrating how biography, history, and social structures combine in intricate and shifting ways. Phillip writes that he learned to listen to community members whose frames differ from his own, affirming their rights to participate while he searched for elements of overlap in which they might form coalitions on specific issues of concern. Phillip explains: "I believe that it is up to us to make wise decisions on how we live, where we live, and how we live with other people in mind" (Kinloch, 2009, p. 38). Throughout the book, Kinloch enables readers to see adolescent students in continuous states of becoming a student, an expert, a leader, a teacher, an activist, and a traveler across physical, cultural, and emotional boundaries.

Phillip's, Khaleeq's, Hartman's, and Kinloch's school and Harlem are not the menacing, dysfunctional, and helpless places often portrayed in the media. Rather, they are communities full of culture, resources, and histories that were currently using reading with sociological imagination in order to struggle with a specific example of complex global practices of acquisition, misrecognition, and misrepresentation.

The two students were remarkably articulate about the role of reading in their learning and lives.

> You gotta read and write. This ain't just about gentrification; it's about reading and writing, figuring out what's going on. You gotta know what they know. (Phillip, cited in Kinloch, 2009, p. 53)
>
> Literacy is who I am, what Harlem is, what Big G (gentrification) is taking away. But with literacy, my word's my weapon. (Khaleeq, cited in Kinloch, 2009, p. 55)

Radical Democratic Reading Education Policy

With the recorded failures of the Reading First Initiative from the No Child Left Behind policy (and its equivalent, the National Reading Strategy, in Great Britain), Brian Street (2012) calls for a "reschooling" of society along the lines that Kinloch described—more informal, fluid, self-directed arrangements in which schools would build on the social practices that students developed outside of classrooms. Schools, then, become one among several sites in which students develop their repertoires of reading practices in order to negotiate their pasts, presents, and futures. Reschooling requires school personnel to acknowledge all communities' ways with words as useful for individuals to meet specific needs and demands. Academic literacies are to be built from students' previous reading and writing practices. Street (2012) considers this move to be a balance between "developing a common set of standards and meeting the diversity of communities and learners" (p. 221), in which the dialectic is permitted to demonstrate its power in both spaces. The social literacy practices learned within communities and other institutions are embraced as what students need to know to enter formal education, and schooling can help inform, articulate, and expand those literacies in ways perhaps unavailable in students' everyday lives.

In 1990 Peter Freebody and Allan Luke first proposed their "four resources model of reading" as a description of "what our culture expects, here and now, from people in their management of text" (Freebody & Luke, 1990, p. 7), and, therefore, as basic standards for any reading education policy. They argued that readers must break the code used to compose any text, determine what the text means, make use of the text, and understand what it does to others and themselves. Although the first two resources appear in most liberal, conservative, and neoliberal definitions of reading, the third and fourth resources—the critical ones—rarely do. Yet in the text-saturated world of the 21st century, the third resource keeps reading always a purposeful social activity and the fourth engages analysis and judgment of the public pedagogy of the producers of the text. All the resources are necessary simultaneously, Freebody and Luke contend; none are more important, and all are catalysts for the others. Citing the earlier work of Street, Freebody and Luke explain that the social context of the reading event will mediate readers' employment of the resources. Home, church, work, play, and schools, therefore, invite different mixes and depths of resources at different times.

In this way, reschooling and the four resources model could map closely onto radical democratic goals for education. Students' reading capabilities vary according to the breadth of individuals' or communities' repertoires of practices, the depth of control exercised, and the disruptive capacities of those practices to the consensus around social norms that create and maintain maldistribution, misrecognition, and misrepresentation. Radical democratic teaching of reading helps individuals and groups build on these capabilities. Success in this teaching is dependent on teachers' commitment to reschooling to be sure, but also on their repertoires of pedagogical practices and their abilities to accommodate differential effects of teaching practices on different groups of students. Through the choices made, teachers will represent what counts as reading, who counts as readers, and where reading might lead. Luke and Freebody (1999) explain: "It was our position that determining how to teach literacy could not be simply scientific, but rather had to involve a moral, political, and cultural decision about the kind of literate practices needed to enhance both people's agency over their life trajectories and communities' intellectual, cultural, and semiotic resources in multimediated economies." According to Street and Luke (Luke, Woods, & Weir, 2013), the challenge is to capture reschooling and the four resources in official policy.

Examples

The Department of Education and Training (2009) of New South Wales, Australia, accepted this challenge. The four resources model has a prominent place in *An Introduction to Quality Literacy Teaching: Explicit, Systemic, Balanced and Integrated*: "The work of Luke and Freebody has provided a model of interrelated literacy resources that has been part of the literature for more than a decade, informing syllabuses, curriculum support materials and professional publications across Australia . . . about two essential cornerstones of quality teaching—balanced and integrated" (Department of Education and Training, 2009, pp. 14–15). K–12 Literacy Standard 1.2.4 states: "Teachers will ensure students are equipped with a range of literacy practices and skills that support them in code-breaking and understanding, using, analyzing and evaluating texts for a variety of purposes and audiences" (Department of Education and Training, 2009, p. 37). To guide interpretation of that standard, the

Introduction to Quality Literacy Teaching devoted two pages (of 40) to explain the resources.

> Code breaking is the ability to break the code of written texts by recognizing and using the fundamental architecture of written language.
> Meaning making is the ability to understand and compose meaningful written, visual, spoken, digital and multimodal texts.
> Text using is the ability to use written, spoken, visual, digital and multimodal texts in functional ways within and outside the school setting.
> Text analyzing is the ability to critically analyse written, spoken, visual, digital and multimodal texts and understand that texts represent particular points of view and influence people's ideas. (p. 18)

When text using and text analyzing are in place, "students are likely to say: I understand what these kinds of texts are used for" and "I know why this text works and how it is trying to make me think, feel, or act" (Department of Education and Training, 2009, p. 19).

The Ontario Language Curriculum "captures the practices of the four resources model" (Secretariat, 2009). According to the Secretariat, the third and fourth resources are not added to literacy programs, but form an essential lens through which teachers can reschool society by (1) "honouring the cultural capital and multiliteracies of all students . . . beginning with and building on the unique identities and diverse community perspectives represented within the classroom and school" (Secretariat, 2009, p. 1), and (2) "engaging students in considering alternative and diverse perspectives—perspectives they may be unaware of, those they might not agree with, those that differ between texts, or points of view that vary from the one presented by a particular author" (Secretariat, 2009, p. 2). The official Ontario standards for reading instruction remind teachers that all texts are the products of many decisions, contain belief and value messages, and serve different interests. "Each medium develops its own language in order to position readers/viewers in certain ways" (Secretariat, 2009, p. 2). In order to support students' decisions about whether to accept the positions texts offer, the Secretariat encourages teachers to engage in problem posing about texts, to juxtapose two texts on the same topic from different ideological positions, and to switch perspectives in order to see another's point of view.

Why Not Here?

Although liberal, conservative, and neoliberal educational pundits rarely mention Australia or Canada, in comparisons of international test scores both countries ranked higher on the 2009 Programme for International Student Assessment (PISA) test of literacy. Canada placed sixth and Australia was ninth. The United States' literacy scores for 15-year-olds rated 17th, near the international mean. Of course, there is no identifiable cause for these differences, but radical democrats hypothesize about the more sophisticated four resources model with its broad definition of text, ties to social practices, and political savvy and argue using the very test scores that preoccupy the discourse surrounding reading education in America. They could point without pride to the difference in poverty rates as well. In 2012, 9.4 percent of Canadians and 12.8 percent of Australians lived in poverty. The American rate was 15.1 percent. Moreover, 11 percent of Australian children, 14 percent of Canadian children, and 22 percent of American children lived below poverty lines. Shifts toward a four resources model in state literacy education policies would not add to the cost of public education. Canada and Australia spend slightly lower percentages of their gross domestic product on education than the United States. If Larry Cuban is correct about educational policy, then, it must be politics that keeps the third and fourth resources from the official educational policies in America.

That is, state legislators and curriculum officials do not find it politically acceptable to invite types of reading that enable students to read with competence *and* imagination. Certainly, they want American students to be code breakers and meaning makers in order to function and compete, but they draw their official lines through text users and analyzers, discouraging practices in classrooms inviting students to question all that they read, to analyze the positions offered them through those texts, and to resist them when the positions deny participatory parity that could lead to redistribution, recognition, and representation outside the acceptable liberal, conservative, or neoliberal boundaries. Liberal education officials can ignore the third and fourth resources publicly because student responses lack scientific evidence of their existence or import. Conservatives find those resources relevant only at the end of public education and only for a few who make it that far. If text using and text analysis were offered too soon to too many, they would undermine the accepted virtues on which the current American consensus is built. Neoliberals consider text use and analysis useful strategies, but only for individuals' adaptation to the challenges of the new global innovation economy. Those are public reasons offered. In private, radical democrats charge that all three groups fear likely changes that would follow a nation of students who graduated from Vivian Vasquez's, Timothy O'Keefe's, and Latoya Hartman's classrooms.

In a special issue of *Theory Into Practice* titled "The Future of Critical Literacies in U.S. Schools," guest editors JuliAnna Avila and Jessica Pandya (2012) acknowledge as much—"critical literacies remain seemingly irrelevant to literacy policymakers" (p. 1). In the hope of catching policy makers' attention with classroom evidence (Alverman, 2012), radical democratic contributors provide classroom, community, and historical data to demonstrate the ongoing importance of critical literacies in the lives of children, youth, and young adults from diverse backgrounds. They show that despite the tactics of teacher accountability for skill and content coverage and nearly continuous testing, some teachers are able to base their literacy instruction on students' significant issues. For example, Avila and Michael Moore (2012) describe a teacher's efforts to infuse Common Core Standards with digital critical literacies. Citing specific standards across reading, writing, speaking, and listening, they present a teacher's pedagogical choice to juxtapose the reading of Martin Luther King Jr.'s "Beyond Vietnam: A Time to Speak" with a newspaper's civil rights timeline that appeared in the local newspaper on the national holiday in his honor. Students—even those that state tests positioned as below basic in proficiency—compared King's ideas with their own lives and disputed the timeline's characterization that many issues of redistribution, recognition, and representation have been settled in America. Avila and Moore (2012) conclude that "although [U.S.] standards will likely never overtly endorse critical literacy . . . the critical aspect is for educators to apply a critical lens to the standards themselves and to help their students do the same" (p. 33).

P. David Pearson (2013) makes a similar claim. In an attempt to draw a grand synthesis of models of reading, Pearson argues that Common Core anchor standards imply the four resources model. The first three anchor standards are directed toward developing readers' resources for breaking text codes. Standards seven, eight, and nine address meaning making and bleed into standards four, five, and six in order to deliver both text using and text analyzing resources. He locates what he labels the "more critical" resources within the verbs used in the final six standards. Readers will delineate, interpret, analyze, assess, integrate, and evaluate words and phrases, text structures, point of view, and arguments presented in print texts primarily, but also in diverse media (standard 7). Pearson acknowledges that the standards and the Common Core movement lack the explicit moral, political, and cultural references of Freebody and Luke's model (or the New South Wales and Ontario treatments), but within the anchor standards, he identifies an opening for individual and groups of radical democratic teachers to build reading curriculum around students' questions and imaginations.

Similar to the contributors to *Theory Into Practice,* Pearson's optimism is tempered by the neoliberal purpose of Common Core—to deliver national markets to entrepreneurs who will invent the solutions to reading problems in the United States. As Gates explained, the success of Common Core will come through the alignment of standards, curriculum, and instruction to be accomplished through national tests and data sharing. To discipline teachers and students into this regime, Common Core officials delineate enabling standards for each anchor from preschool to high school graduation, instruct publishers how to prepare materials appropriately for each grade, and provide instructional models that encourage the notion that meaning is found in the text (and not the transaction of reading, text, and activity within a historical/political context). To enforce that discipline, federal officials insisted on test scores as part of teacher and school personnel evaluations in order for states to qualify for Race to the Top funds. Like Margie and the others at the bingo hall, the rich, business, and the government stack the odds against radical democratic teachers and the communities they serve.

Radical democrats understand poverty as a nexus of economic, social, cultural, political, and ecological relations that have no single identifiable cause beyond a societal tolerance for inequality and exclusion. They reject the ideological consensus that the poor are deficient, lazy, or losers, and seek to disrupt the institutional instantiations of this consensus that enforces maldistribution, misrecognition, and misrepresentation, limiting the poor from participatory parity in society. Rather, radical democrats recognize that the poor are composed of diverse individuals with multiple and fluid identities, and that they are located within spaces affording them various sets of opportunities and limits. Therefore, they appreciate the poor as the ones who know the most about the specificity of their daily struggles and who should name the sites for substantive action toward remedies. Schooling in general and reading education in particular become the continued development and extension of individuals' home and community reading practices to enable them to identify the way things are, to understand the positions offered to them, and to imagine how they could be different. Rather than a search for a new consensus, radical democratic teachers seek to harness the power of difference, agonism, and temporary coalitions with eyes toward reflexive justice.

Reading poverty in America is an urgent need and a continuous struggle. The Great Recession made visible the possibilities of falling and improbabilities of rising among social classes that had been hidden from view since the 1980s. Since the Great Recession's official end in 2009:

> The incomes of the top 1 percent of citizens rose over 30 percent, while the real income of the bottom 40 percent fell by 6 percent.
> Among industrialized nations, Americans are the least likely to have upward economic mobility.
> More African American males are now in the criminal justice system than were slaves in American history.
> Despite a near doubling of the Americans eligible for food assistance (SNAP), the program's $4.45 per day average allotment and its roles will be cut.
> The Supreme Court ruled that campaign contributions were free speech and, therefore, no limits could be placed on corporations', associations', or labor unions' donations to political parties.
> Article 5 of the Civil Rights Act of 1965 was ruled unconstitutional, and subsequently Texas and North Carolina legislators passed voter identification laws (to prevent nonexistent fraud).

We face decisions about how we wish to live together and what positions we will assume as those decisions are made. In modern society, "individuals should have the possibility to organize their lives as they wish, to choose their own ends, and to realize them as they think best" (Mouffe, 1996, p. 20), however, there is nothing in that society—not even in the U.S. Constitution—that guarantees the existence of a middle class, the acceptance of cultural differences, or the promise of universal enfranchisement. Those became possibilities in America because coalitions of individuals read the way things were/are and imagined that together—around issues of redistribution, recognition, and representation—they could extend participatory parity among all citizens. Obviously, that work is not complete and never will be as new identities emerge. Only the radical democrats offer teachers and citizens this type of reading to continue the constant struggle for reflexive justice in our imperfect democracy.

> Nothing good happens in Washington, or for that matter, in state capitals, unless good people outside Washington and those state capitals make it happen. Unless they push very hard. Unless they're organized, mobilized, and energized to force the political system to respond. (Robert Reich as quoted in Cook, 2012, p. 36)

REFERENCES

Aaron, H. (2013). Progressives and the safety net. *Democracy: A Journal of Ideas, 27*. Retrieved 9/24/13 from www.democracyjournal.org/27/progressives-and-the-safety-net.php?page=all

Achieve. (2004). Ready or not: Creating a high school diploma that counts. Retrieved 12/9/13 from www.google.com/url?sa=t&rct=j&q=&esrc=s&source=web&cd=1&ved=0CCsQFjAA&url=http%3A%2F%2Fwww.achieve.org%2FReadyorNot&ei=RzGmUtWNFKqnsQT5w4HYAQ&usg=AFQjCNH_p-Qls0A2-4rDWeeuH5mIGT8cVg&bvm=bv.57752919,d.cWc

Acs, G., & Turner, M. (2008). Making work pay enough. *A new safety net for low income families paper 1*. Washington, DC: Urban Institute. Retrieved 9/24/13 from www.urban.org/UploadedPDF/411710_work_pay.pdf

Adams, M. (1990). *Beginning to read: Thinking and learning about print*. Cambridge, MA: MIT Press.

Adams, R. (2012, April 18). David Lindsay-Abraire's good people: The American theater rediscovers class. World Socialist website. Retrieved 9/23/13 from www.wsws.org/en/articles/2012/04/good-a18.html

Addy, S., Engelhart, W., & Skinner, C. (2013, January 30). Basic facts about low-income children. National Center for Children in Poverty. Columbia University, New York. Retrieved 9/25/13 from www.nccp.org/publications/pub_1074.html.

Allen, T. (2012, October 9). Paul Ryan hefts the white man's burden. *In These Times*. Retrieved 12/20/13 from http://inthesetimes.com/article/13974/paul_ryan_hefts_white_mans_burden/

Allington, R. (2002). *Big brother and the national reading curriculum*. Portsmouth, NH: Heinemann.

Alterman, E. (2002). *What liberal media: The truth about bias and the news*. New York: Basic.

Alverman, D. (2012). Afterward. *Theory Into Practice, 51*, 62–67.

Anatani, Y., Chau, M., Wight, V., & Addy, S. (2011, November). Rent burden, housing subsidies and the well being of children and youth. National Center for Children in Poverty. Columbia University, New York. Retrieved 9/27/13 from www.nccp.org/publications/pub_1043.html

References

Anderson, R., Hiebert, E., Scott, J., & Wilkerson, I. (1985). *Becoming a nation of readers.* Washington, DC: National Institute of Education.

Armor, D., & Sousa, S. (2012). Restoring a true safety net. *National Affairs, 13.* Retrieved 9/24/13 from www.nationalaffairs.com/publications/detail/restoring-a-true-safety-net

Au, K. (2011). *Literacy achievement and diversity.* New York: Teachers College.

Avila, J., & Moore, M. (2012). Critical literacy, digital literacies, and common core state standards: A workable union? *Theory Into Practice, 51,* 27–33.

Avila, J., & Pandya, J. (Eds.). (2012). The future of critical literacies in U.S. schools. *Theory Into Practice, 51,* 1–67.

Barnett, W. S. (2010). *Thoughts on the state of preschool: Preschool today.* National Institute for Early Education Research. New York. Retrieved 9/26/13 from http://preschoolmatters.org/2010/05/04/steven-barnett-thoughts-on-the-state-of-preschool/

Barnett, W. S., Carolan, M., Fitzgerald, J., & Squires, J. (2013). *The state of preschool 2012 yearbook.* New Brunswick, NJ: National Institute for Early Education Research. Retrieved 9/25/13 from http://nieer.org/sites/nieer/files/yearbook2012.pdf

Beeghley, L. (2004). *The structure of social stratification in the United States.* New York: Pearson.

Bell, T. (1986). Education policy development in the Reagan administration. *Phi Delta Kappan, 68,* 485–490.

Bennett, W. (1988). *James Madison elementary school: A curriculum for American schools.* Washington, DC: Government Printing Office.

Bennett, W. (1994). *The book of virtues.* New York: Simon & Schuster.

Bennett, W. (1995a). *The moral compass.* New York: Simon & Schuster.

Bennett, W. (1995b). *The children's book of virtues.* New York: Simon & Schuster.

Bennett, W., Finn, C., & Cribb, J. (1999). *The educated child.* New York: Free Press.

Bentele, K. (2012, April 30). *Evaluating the performance of the U.S. social safety net in the great recession.* Center for Social Policy. University of Massachusetts, Boston. Retrieved 9/24/13 from http://scholarworks.umb.edu/cgi/viewcontent.cgi?article=1061&context=csp_pubs

Berliner, D. (2009, March). *Poverty and potential: Out of school factors and school success.* Education Policy Research Unit. Boulder, CO. Retrieved 9/24/13 from http://nepc.colorado.edu/publication/poverty-and-potential

Bernstein, J., Chollet, D., & Peterson, S. (2010, April). Does insurance coverage improve health outcomes? *Mathematica Policy Research, 1.* Retrieved 9/26/13 from www.mathematica-mpr.com/publications/PDFs/health/reformhealthcare_IB1.pdf

Berube, A., Kneebone, E., & Nadeau, C. (2011, November 3). The re-emergence of concentrated poverty. *Metropolitan Opportunity Series, 23.* Brookings Institute. Retrieved 9/25/13 from www.brookings.edu/research/papers/2011/11/03-poverty-kneebone-nadeau-berube

Bloom, A. (1987). *The closing of the American mind.* New York: Simon & Schuster.

Bracey, G. (2009). *The Bracey report on the condition of public education.* National Education Policy Center. Boulder, CO. Retrieved 9/25/13 from www.google.com/url?sa=t&rct=j&q=&esrc=s&source=web&cd=2&ved=0CDUQFjAB&url=http%3A%2F%2Fnepc.colorado.edu%2Fpublication%2Fbracey-report&ei=QiWmUtSkKsfgsATVrQI&usg=AFQjCNGu2v0jOwsx5aHqJB3Hk-Oj-dYQpg&bvm=bv.57752919,d.cWc

Brantley, B. (2011, March 3). Been back to the old neighborhood? *New York Times.* Retrieved 9/23/13 from http://theater2.nytimes.com/2011/03/04/theater/reviews/04good.html?pagewanted=all&_r=0

Bravve, E., Bolton, M., Couch, L., & Crowley, S. (2012, March). *Out of reach 2012: America's forgotten housing crisis.* National Low Income Coalition. Washington, DC. Retrieved 9/24/13 from http://nlihc.org/sites/default/files/oor/2012-OOR.pdf

References

Brighouse, H., & Schouten, G. (2011). Understanding the context for existing reform and research proposals. In G. Duncan & R. Murnane (Eds.), *Whither opportunity? Rising inequality, schools, and children's life chances* (pp. 507–522). New York: Russell Sage Foundation.

Brooks, D. (2013, February 14). When families fail. *New York Times*. Retrieved from www.nytimes.com/2013/02/15/opinion/brooks-crayons-to-college.html

Bryk, A., Sebring, P., Allensworth, E., Luppescu, S., & Easton, J. (2010). *Organizing schools for improvement: Lessons from Chicago*. Cambridge, MA: Harvard Education Press.

Buckley, W. F. (1955, November). Our mission statement. *National Review, 1*. Retrieved 9/25/13 from www.nationalreview.com/articles/223549/our-mission-statement/william-f-buckley-jr

Calfee, R. (2013). Knowledge, evidence, and faith: How the federal government used science to take over public schools. In K. Goodman, R. Calfee, & Y. Goodman (Eds.), *Whose knowledge counts in government literacy policies?* New York: Routledge.

Calfee, R., & Drum, P. (Eds.). (1979). *Teaching reading in compensatory reading classes*. Newark, DE: International Reading Association.

Carnine, D. (1999). Campaigns for moving research into practice. *Remedial and Special Education, 20,* 2–6, 35.

Center for Budget and Policy Priorities. (2013, January 25). *Policy basics: Introduction to public housing*. Retrieved 9/25/13 from www.cbpp.org/cms/index.cfm?fa=view&id=2528

Center for Disease Control and Prevention. (2012, April 17). *Reproductive and birth outcomes*. Retrieved 9/26/13 from http://ephtracking.cdc.gov/showRbLBWGrowthRetardationEnv.action

Centers for Medicare and Medicaid Services. (2011). *CHIP participation*. Retrieved 9/26/13 from www.medicaid.gov/Medicaid-CHIP-Program-Information/By-Topics/Childrens-Health-Insurance-Program-CHIP/Childrens-Health-Insurance-Program-CHIP.html

Chau, M., Thampi, K., & Wight, V. (2010, October). Basic facts about low-income children, Children under age 18. National Center for Children in Poverty. Columbia University, New York. Retrieved 9/26/13 from www.nccp.org/publications/pdf/download_364.pdf

Cheadle, J., & Goosby, B. (2010). Birth weight, cognitive development, and life chances. *Social Science Research, 29,* 570–584.

Children's Defense Fund. (2013). *Children in the states: Fact Sheets 2013*. Washington, DC. Retrieved 9/26/13 from www.childrensdefense.org/child-research-data-publications/data/state-data-repository/children-in-the-states.html

Citro, C., & Michael, R. (1995). *Measuring poverty: A new approach*. Panel on Poverty and Family Assistance. Committee on National Statistics. Washington, DC: National Academy Press. Retrieved 9/26/13 from www.nap.edu/openbook.php?isbn=0309051282

Coleman, D. (2011, April). *As quoted in School Matters: David Coleman's global revenge and the common core*. Retrieved 9/27/13 from www.schoolsmatter.info/2012/04/david-colemans-global-revenge-and.html

Coleman, D. (2012). *Common core in ELA: An overview*. Retrieved 9/27/13 from www.engageny.org/resource/common-core-in-ela-literacy-an-overview

Coleman-Jensen, A., Nord, M., Andrews, M., & Carlson, S. (2012, September). *Household food security in the United States in 2011*. Economic Research Service, Report 141. United States Department of Agriculture. Retrieved 9/26/13 from www.ers.usda.gov/media/884525/err141.pdf

Collaboration for Poverty Research. (2010). *Poverty and stress*. Retrieved 9/27/13 from www.stanford.edu/group/scspi/cpr/cpr_lab_poverty_and_stress.html

Committee of Fifteen. (1895). *Report of the committee of fifteen on elementary education with the reports of the sub-committees: On the training of teachers; on the correlation of studies in elementary education; on the organization of city school systems.* Retrieved 9/27/13 from http://archive.org/details/committelemedu00natirich

Committee of Ten. (1893). *Report of the committee of ten on secondary school studies.* Retrieved 12/2013 from http://books.google.com/books?id=PfcBAAAAYAAJ&pg=PA3&lpg=PA3#v=onepage&q&f=false

Common Core State Standards Initiative. (2010). *Myths vs. facts.* Retrieved 9/27/13 from www.corestandards.org/resources/myths-vs-facts

Common Core State Standards Initiative. (2013). Frequently asked questions. Retrieved 12/20/13 from www.corestandards.org/resources/frequently-asked-questions

Common Core Validation Committee. (2010, June). *Reaching higher: The common core state standards validation committee.* National Governors Association, Council of Chief State School Officers. Retrieved 9/27/13 from www.corestandards.org/assets/CommonCoreReport_6.10.pdf

Compton-Lilly, C., Rogers, R., & Lewis, T. (2012). Analyzing epistemological considerations related to diversity: An integrative critical literature review of family literacy scholarship. *Reading Research Quarterly, 47,* 33–60.

Cook, C. (2012, November). The Progressive interview with Robert Reich. *The Progressive, 76,* 11, 36.

Council on Foreign Relations. (2012). *U.S. education reform and national security.* Task Force Report. Retrieved 9/25/13 from www.cfr.org/united-states/us-education-reform-national-security/p27618

Counts, G. (1932). *Dare the schools build a new social order?* New York: John Day.

Crotty, J. (2013, August 16). Is common core too hardcore? *Forbes.* Retrieved 9/24/13 from www.forbes.com/sites/jamesmarshallcrotty/2013/08/16/is-common-core-too-hard-core/

Cuban, L. (2010, July 25). *Common core standards: Hardly an evidence based policy.* Larry Cuban on school reform and classroom practice. Retrieved 9/27/13 from http://larrycuban.wordpress.com/2010/07/25/common-core-standards-hardly-an-evidence-based-policy/

Cummins, J. (2007). Pedagogies for the poor? Re-aligning reading instruction for low-income students with scientifically based reading research. *Educational Researcher, 36,* 564–572.

Cunningham, J. (2001). The national reading panel report. *Reading Research Quarterly, 36,* 326–335.

Currier, E. (2012, July 9). *Pursuing the American dream: Economic mobility across generations.* Pew Charitable Trust Report. Retrieved 9/26/13 from www.pewstates.org/research/reports/pursuing-the-american-dream-85899403228

Curto, V., Fryer, R., & Howard, M. (2011). It may not take a village: Increasing achievement among the poor. In G. Duncan & R. Murnane (Eds.), *Whither opportunity? Rising inequality, schools, and children's life chances* (pp. 483–506). New York: Russell Sage Foundation.

Deparle, J., & Gebeloff, R. (2010, January 3). Living on nothing but food stamps. *New York Times.* Retrieved 9/24/13 from www.nytimes.com/2010/01/03/us/03foodstamps.html?pagewanted=all

Deparle, J., Gebeloff, R., & Tavernise, S. (2011, November 18). Older, suburban and struggling, "near poor" startle the census. *New York Times.* Retrieved 9/24/13 from www.nytimes.com/2011/11/19/us/census-measures-those-not-quite-in-poverty-but-struggling.html?pagewanted=all

References

Department of Education and Training. (2009). *An introduction to quality literacy teaching: Explicit, systematic, balanced and integrated.* New South Wales, Australia. Retrieved 9/24/13 from www.decd.sa.gov.au/northernadelaide/files/links/An_Introduction_to_Quality.pdf

Dewey, J. (1916). *Democracy and education.* New York: John Day.

Dropkin, R., & Tobier, A. (Eds.). (1975). *Roots of open education in America.* New York: Workshop Center for Open Education

Drum, K. (2011, April). Plutocracy now. *Mother Jones, 36*(7), 22–28, 63.

Duncan, A. (2011, April 20). U.S. Secretary of Education Arne Duncan (public address). Woodrow Wilson School of Public and International Affairs, Princeton University. Princeton, NJ. Retrieved 9/24/13 from www.youtube.com/watch?v=aWrXmbPb91E

Duncan, A. (2013, August 19). Statement by U.S. Secretary of Education Arne Duncan on Tennessee making changes to teacher licensure policy. U.S. Department of Education, Washington DC. Retrieved 9/27/13 from www.ed.gov/news/press-releases/statement-ussecretary-education-arne-duncan-tennessee-making-changes-teacher-li

Duncan, G., & Murnane, R. (Eds.). (2011). *Whither opportunity? Rising inequality, schools, and children's life chances.* New York: Russell Sage Foundation.

Edelman, P. (2012). *So rich, so poor: Why it's so hard to end poverty in America.* New York: New Press.

Elementary and Secondary Education Act. (1965). Retrieved 12/20/13 from https://sites.google.com/site/publicedforparents/original-text-of-1965-esea-act

Engelmann, S. (1992). *War against schools: Academic child abuse.* New York: Halycon House.

Evans, G., & Schamberg, M. (2009). Childhood poverty, chronic stress, and adult working memory. *Proceedings of the National Academy of Science (early edition).* Retrieved 9/25/13 from www.pnas.org/content/early/2009/03/27/0811910106.abstract

Evans, M.S. (1960). *The Sharon statement.* Retrieved 9/24/13 from www2.fiu.edu/~yaf/sharon.html

FactCheck.org. (2013, February 20). Obama's preschool stretch. Retrieved 12/9/13 from www.google.com/url?sa=t&rct=j&q=&esrc=s&source=web&cd=1&ved=0CCsQFjAA&url=http%3A%2F%2Fwww.factcheck.org%2F2013%2F02%2Fobamas-preschool-stretch%2F&ei=WC6mUsTsHM_lsASA2YLYCw&usg=AFQjCNE86COB8i449xEPLznjxVQCx9eAWQ&bvm=bv.57752919,d.cWc

Farah, M., Shera, D., Savae, J. Betancourt, L., Giannetta, J., Brodsky, N., Malmud, E., & Hunt, H. (2006). Childhood poverty: Specific association with neurocognitive development. *Brain Research, 1110,* 166–174. Retrieved 9/27/13 from www.psych.upenn.edu/~mfarah/Development-povertyassociation.pdf

Fass, P. (2009, April). *Measuring poverty in the United States: Fact sheet.* National Center for Children in Poverty. Columbia University, New York. Retrieved 9/26/13 from www.nccp.org/publications/pdf/text_876.pdf

Federal Education Budget Project. (2013). *Federal school nutrition programs.* New America Foundation. Washington, DC. Retrieved 9/26/13 from http://febp.newamerica.net/background-analysis/federal-school-nutrition-programs

Finkelstein, A., Taubman, S., Wright, B., Bernstein, M., Gruber, J., Newhouse, J., Allen, H., & Baicker, K. (2011). *The Oregon health insurance experiment.* National Bureau of Economic Research. Cambridge, MA. Retrieved 9/26/13 from www.nber.org/programs/ag/rrc/NB10–14%20Baicker,%20Finkelstein%20et%20al%20FINAL.pdf

Fraser, N. (2009). *Scales of justice: Reimagining political space in a globalizing world.* New York: Columbia University.

References

Freebody, P., & Luke, A. (1990). Literacies programs: Debates and demands in cultural context. *Prospect: An Australian Journal of TESOL, 5,* 7–16.

Friedman, T. (2012, January 3). So much fun. So irrelevant. *New York Times.* Retrieved 9/24/13 from www.nytimes.com/2012/01/04/opinion/friedman-so-much-fun-so-irrelevant.html

Gabe, T. (2012, September 27). *Poverty in the United States: 2011.* Congressional Research Service Report for Congress. Retrieved 9/26/13 from www.fas.org/sgp/crs/misc/RL33069.pdf

Gamse, B., Bonlay, B., Fountain, A., Unlu, F., Maree, K., McCall, T., & McCormack, R. (2011). *Reading first implementation study 2008–2009.* U.S. Department of Education. Retrieved 9/24/13 from www2.ed.gov/about/offices/list/opepd/ppss/reports.html#reading

Gates, B. (2009, July 21). *Address to the national conference of state legislatures.* Retrieved 9/27/13 from www.gatesfoundation.org/media-center/speeches/2009/07/bill-gates-national-conference-of-state-legislatures-ncsl

Gee, J. (1992). What is literacy? In P. Shannon (Ed.), *Becoming political.* Portsmouth, NH: Heinemann.

Gee, J. (2008). A sociocultural perspective on opportunity to learn. In P. Moss (Ed.), *Assessment, equity and opportunity.* New York: Cambridge.

Gilbert, D. (2002). *American class structure in an age of growing inequality.* New York: Wadsworth.

Gillette, M. (1996). *Launching the war on poverty: An oral history.* New York: Twayne.

Glynn, S. (2012, April 16). *The gender wage gap double whammy.* Center for American Progress. Retrieved 9/25/13 from www.americanprogress.org/issues/women/news/2012/04/16/11428/the-gender-wage-gap-double-whammy/

Goldin, C., & Katz, L. (2008). *The race between education and technology.* Cambridge, MA: Belknap.

Goodnough, A. (2013 August 14). Helping the uninsured find coverage. *New York Times.* Retrieved 9/26/13 from www.nytimes.com/2013/08/15/us/politics/the-challenge-of-helping-the-uninsured-find-coverage.html

Harrington, M. (1962). *The other America.* New York: Macmillan.

Hart, B., & Risley, T. (1995). *Meaningful differences in the everyday experiences of young American children.* Baltimore, MD: Brookes.

Haskins, R. (2006, March 15). *Welfare reform: Success or failure? It worked.* Brookings Institute. Washington, DC. Retrieved 9/26/13 from www.brookings.edu/research/articles/2006/03/15welfare-haskins

Haskins, R. (2012, April 17). *Testimony of Ron Haskins before the Committee on the Budget, U.S. House of Representatives.* Retrieved 9/24/13 from http://budget.house.gov/uploadedfiles/haskinstestimony4172012.pdf

Hawkridge, D., Albert, C., Chalupsky, C., & Roberts, O. (1968). *A study of selected programs for the disadvantaged. Part 1.* Palo Alto, CA: American Institute for Research in the Behavioral Sciences.

Hayek, F. (1944/2007). *The road to serfdom with intellectuals and socialism.* Chicago, IL: University of Chicago.

Head Start. (2012, October). *Third grade follow-up to the Head Start impact study, final report.* Office of Planning, Research and Evaluation. Department of Health and Human Services. Retrieved 9/27/13 from www.acf.hhs.gov/sites/default/files/opre/head_start_report.pdf

Heath, S. B. (1983). *Ways with words.* New York: Cambridge.

Heckman, L., Moon, S., Pinto, R., Savelyev, P., & Yavitz, A. (2010). The rate of return to the Perry High/Scope preschool program. *Journal of Public Economy, 94,* 114–128.

References

Heillig, J., & Jez, S. (2010). *Teach for America: A review of the evidence.* Boulder, CO: National Education and Policy Center. Retrieved from http://nepc.colorado.edu/files/PB-TeachAmerica-Heilig.pdf

Heller, W. (1964, January 13). The problem of poverty in America. In *The annual report of the Council of Economic Advisors.* Submitted to President Johnson. Retrieved 9/27/13 from fraser.stlouisfed.org/docs/publications/ERP/1964/ERP_ARCEA_1964.pdf

Herrnstein, R., & Murray, C. (1995). *The bell curve: Intelligence and social class in American life.* New York: Free Press.

Hess, F. (2010). *The same thing over and over: How school reformers get stuck in yesterday's ideas.* Cambridge, MA: Harvard.

Hiebert, E., & Van Sluys, K. (2013). Examining three assumptions about text complexity. In K. Goodman, R. Calfee, & Y. Goodman (Eds.), *Whose knowledge counts in government literacy policies?* New York: Routledge.

Hill, P. (2005, October 5). Re-creating public education in New Orleans. *Education Week, 25.* Retrieved 9/27/13 from www.edweek.org/chat/2005/10/05/transcript_10_05_2005.html

House, E., Glass, G., McLean, L., & Walker, D. (1978). No simple answer: Critique of the follow through evaluation. *Harvard Educational Review, 28,* 128–160.

Hud.gov. (2013). Retrieved from http://portal.hud.gov/hudportal/HUD?src=/program_offices/public_indian_housing/programs/hcv/about/fact_sheet

Huey, E. B. (1908/1968). *The psychology and pedagogy of reading.* Cambridge, MA: MIT.

Hull, G., & Moje, E. (2012). What is the development of literacy the development of? Understanding Language. Stanford University. Retrieved 9/23/13 from http://ell.stanford.edu/sites/default/files/pdf/academic-papers/05-Hull%20%26%20Moje%20CC%20Paper%20FINAL.pdf

Hurley, R. (1969). *Poverty and mental retardation: A causal relationship.* New York: Vintage.

Issacs, J. (2012, March). *Starting school at a disadvantage: The school readiness of poor children.* Center on Children and Families. Brookings Institute. Retrieved 9/24/13 from www.brookings.edu/research/papers/2012/03/19-school-disadvantage-isaacs

Issacs, J., Sawhill, I., & Haskins, R. (2008). *Getting ahead or losing ground: Economic mobility in America.* Washington, DC: Brookings Institute.

Kaiser Family State Health Facts. (2012). Retrieved 9/26/13 from http://kff.org/statedata/

Kaufman, G. (2013). This week in poverty: An anti-poverty contract for 2013. *The Nation.* Retrieved 9/27/13 from www.thenation.com/blog/172287/week-poverty-antipoverty-contract-2013#

Kaushal, N., Magnuson, K., & Waldgogel, J. (2011). How is family income related to investments in children's learning. In G. Duncan & R. Murnane (Eds.), *Whither opportunity? Rising inequality, schools, and children's life chances* (pp. 187–206). New York: Russell Sage Foundation.

Kay, K. (2010). 21st century skills: Why they matter, what they are, and how we get there. In J. Bellanca & R. Brandt (Eds.), *21st Century skills: Rethinking how students learn.* Bloomington, IN: Solution Tree.

Kennedy, J. F. (1960). Accepting the New York State liberal party nomination. Retrieved 9/27/13 from www.pbs.org/wgbh/americanexperience/features/primary-resources/jfk-nyliberal/

Keppel, F. (1965). *Aid to elementary and secondary education: Hearings before the general subcommittee on education of the committee on education and labor, 89th Congress, 1st session.* Washington, DC: Government Printing Office.

King Jr., M. L. (1967). *Where do we go from here? Community or chaos.* Boston, MA: Beacon.

Kinloch, V. (2009). *Harlem on our minds: Place, race and the literacies of urban youth*. New York: Teachers College.

Klein, A. (2010, February 22). Obama plan would tie Title 1 to college-career standards. *Education Week*. Retrieved 9/27/13 from www.edweek.org/ew/articles/2010/02/22/23esea_ep.h29.html

Kneebone, E., & Garr, E. (2010). *The suburbanization of poverty: Trends in metropolitan America 2000 to 2008*. Metropolitan Policy Program, Brookings Institute. Retrieved 9/2613 from www.brookings.edu/~/media/research/files/papers/2010/1/20%20poverty%20kneebone/0120_poverty_paper.pdf

Krashen, S., Lee, S., & McQuillan, J. (2010). An analysis of PIRLS 2006 data. *California Library Association Journal, 34*, 26–28. Retrieved 9/25/13 from www.ala.org/aasl/sites/ala.org.aasl/files/content/aaslissues/advocacy/Krashen_Lee_McQuillan_PIRLS.pdf

Kristof, N. (2012, December 7). Profiting from a child's illiteracy. *New York Times*. Retrieved 9/24/13 from www.nytimes.com/2012/12/09/opinion/sunday/kristof-profiting-from-a-childs-illiteracy.html?pagewanted=all

Kristol, W. (2013, January 18). What is the future of conservatism? Latinos Ready to Vote. Retrieved 9/27/13 from http://latinosreadytovote.com/william-kristol-what-is-the-future-of-conservatism-2/

Kuriansky, J. (2013). The basic economic security tables for the United States. Wider opportunities for women. Retrieved 9/25/13 from www.wowonline.org/wp-content/uploads/2013/06/Basic-Economic-Security-Table-for-the-United-States-2013-Selected-Families.jpg

Ladd, H., & Fiske, E. (2011, December 11). Class matters. Why won't we admit it? *New York Times*. Retrieved 9/24/13 from www.nytimes.com/2011/12/12/opinion/the-unaddressed-link-between-poverty-and-education.html?pagewanted=all&_r=0

Lagemann, E. C. (2000). *An elusive science: The troubling history of education research*. Chicago, IL: University of Chicago.

Lakoff, G. (2006). *Thinking points: Communicating our American values and vision*. New York: Farrar, Strauss & Giroux.

Lareau, A. (2003). *Unequal childhoods: Class, race, and family life*. Berkeley, CA: University of California Press.

Lareau, A. (2011). *Unequal childhoods: Class, race, and family life* (2nd ed.). Berkeley, CA: University of California Press.

Lee, J. (2006). *Tracking achievement gaps and assessing the impact of NCLB on the gap*. Cambridge, MA: Civil Rights Project of Harvard University.

Lemann, N. (1988, December). The unfinished war. *The Atlantic Online*. Retrieved 9/27/13 from www.theatlantic.com/past/politics/poverty/lemunf1.htm

Lemert, C. (2008). *Social things: An introduction to the sociological life* (4th ed.). Lanham, MD: Rowman & Littlefield.

Lewin, T. (2010, July 21). Many states adopt national standards for their schools. *New York Times*. Retrieved 9/27/13 from www.nytimes.com/2010/07/21/education/21standards.html

Lindsay-Abaire, D. (2012). *Good people*. New York: Dramatist's Play Service.

Locke, J. (1689/1986). *Second treatise of civil government*. Amherst, NY: Prometheus.

Loveless, T. (2012). *How well are American students learning?* The Brown Center Report on American Education. Washington, DC: Brookings Institute. Retrieved 9/25/13 from www.brookings.edu/~/media/newsletters/0216_brown_education_loveless.pdf

Luhby, T. (2012, September 23). Poverty pervades the suburbs. *CNN Money*. Retrieved 9/25/13 from http://money.cnn.com/2011/09/23/news/economy/poverty_suburbs/index.htm

References

Luke, A., & Freebody, P. (1999). Further notes on the four resources model. *Reading Online.* Retrieved 9/24/13 from www.readingonline.org/research/lukefreebody.html

Luke, A., Woods, A., & Weir, K. (Eds.). (2013). *Curriculum, syllabus design and equity.* New York: Routledge.

Marsh, J. (2011). *Class dismissed: Why we cannot teach or learn our way out of inequality.* New York: Monthly Review.

Marshall, R., & Tucker, M. (1992). *Thinking for a living: Work, skills and the future of the American economy.* New York: Basic.

McLaughlin, M. (1975). *Evaluation and reform: The elementary and secondary education act of 1965, Title 1.* Rand Education Policy. New York: Harper Collins.

Mettler, S. (2011). *The submerged state: How invisible government policies undermine American democracy.* Chicago, IL: University of Chicago Press.

Mills, C. W. (1959). *The sociological imagination.* Chicago, IL: University of Chicago.

Mills, H., Jennings, L., Donnelly, A., & Mueller, L. (2001). When teachers have time to talk: The value of curricular conversations. *Language Arts, 79,* 20–28.

Mills, H., Stephens, D., & O'Keefe, T. (2004). Theory in practice: The legacy of Louise Rosenblatt. *Language Arts, 82,* 47–55.

Moats, L. (2008). *Whole language high jinks.* Washington, DC: Thomas Fordham Foundation.

Mooney, C. (2005). *The republican war on science.* New York: Basic.

Morin, R., Taylor, P., & Patten, E. (2012, December 18). *Bipartisan nation of beneficiaries: Social and demographic trends.* Pew Research Center. Retrieved 9/26/13 from www.pewsocialtrends.org/files/2012/12/Benefits_FINAL_12–20.pdf

Mother Jones. (2012, September 19). Full transcript of the Mitt Romney secret video. Retrieved 12/20/13 from www.motherjones.com/politics/2012/09/full-transcript-mitt-romney-secret-video

Mouffe, C. (1996). Radical democracy or liberal democracy. In D. Trend (Ed.), *Radical democracy* (pp. 19–27). New York: Routledge.

Mouffe, C. (2007). Artistic activism and agonistic spaces. *Art and Research: A Journal of Ideas, Contexts and Methods.* Retrieved 9/27/13 from www.artandresearch.org.uk/v1n2/mouffe.html

Mouffe, C. (2009). *Democratic paradox.* New York: Verso.

Murray, C. (1984). *Losing ground: American social policy, 1950–1980.* New York: Basic.

Murray, C. (2012). *Coming apart: The state of white America, 1960–2010.* New York: Crown.

Murray, C. (2013, February 20). The shaky science behind universal pre-K. *Bloomberg View.* Retrieved 9/27/13 from www.bloomberg.com/news/2013–02–21/the-shaky-science-behind-obama-s-universal-pre-k.html

National Center for Education Statistics. (2012). Concentration of public school students eligible for free and reduced price lunch. *Section: School characteristics and climate.* Retrieved 9/26/13 from http://nces.ed.gov/programs/coe/pdf/coe_clb.pdf

National Center for Law and Economic Justice. (2013, September). *Poverty in the United States: A snapshot.* Retrieved 9/26/13 from www.nclej.org/poverty-in-the-us.php

The National Commission on Excellence in Education. (1983). *A nation at risk.* Retrieved 9/24/13 from http://datacenter.spps.org/uploads/sotw_a_nation_at_risk_1983.pdf

National Reading Panel (NRP). (2000). *Teaching children to read.* National Institute of Child Health and Human Development. Washington, DC. Retrieved 9/27/13 from www.nationalreadingpanel.org/publications/summary.htm

Nelson, C., & Sheridan, M. (2011). Lessons from neuroscience research for understanding causal links between family and neighborhood characteristics and educational outcomes.

In G. Duncan & R. Murnane (Eds.), *Whither opportunity? Rising inequality, schools, and children's life chances* (pp. 91–116). New York: Russell Sage Foundation.

Neuman, S., & Celano, D. (2012). *Giving our children a fighting chance: Poverty, literacy and the development of information capital*. New York: Teachers College.

Neuman, S., & Gambrell, L. (Eds.). (2013). *Quality reading instruction in the age of common core standards* (pp. 276–301). Newark: DE: International Reading Association.

New York's common core test scores. (2013, August 7). *New York Times*. Retrieved 9/24/13 from www.nytimes.com/2013/08/08/opinion/new-yorks-common-core-test-scores.html

Nisbett, R. (2009). *Intelligence and how to get it: Why schools and culture count*. New York: Norton.

Noah, T. (2012). *The great divergence: America's growing inequality crisis and what we can do about it*. New York: Bloomsbury.

Noble, K., Norman, M., & Farrah, M. (2005). Neurocognitive correlates of socioeconomic status in kindergarten children. *Development Science, 8*, 74–87. Retrieved 9/27/13 from www.cumc.columbia.edu/dept/sergievsky/fs/publications/Noble-et-al-2005–2.pdf

Nord, M., & Parker, L. (2010). How adequately are food needs of children in low-income households being met? *Children and Youth Services Review, 32*, 1175–1185. Retrieved 9/27/13 from www.sciencedirect.com/science/journal/01907409/32/9

Obama, B. (2010, February 22). Address to the National Governors Association. Washington, DC. Retrieved 2/27/13 from www.gpo.gov/fdsys/pkg/DCPD-201000114/pdf/DCPD-201000114.pdf

Obama, B. (2012, May 7). Presidential proclamation—National charter schools week, 2012. Retrieved 9/27/13 from www.whitehouse.gov/the-press-office/2012/05/07/presidential-proclamation-national-charter-schools-week-2012

Obama, B. (2013, February 12). State of the union address. Washington, DC. Retrieved 9/27/13 from www.nytimes.com/2013/02/13/us/politics/obamas-2013-state-of-the-union-address.html?pagewanted=all

Organization of Economic Cooperation and Development. (2012). *Child poverty*. Retrieved from www.oecd.org/education/CN%20-%20United%20States.pdf

Partnership for 21st Century Skills. (2013). Homepage. Retrieved 9/25/13 from www.p21.org

Payne, C. (2008). *So much reform, so little change: The persistence of failure in urban schools*. Cambridge, MA: Harvard.

Payne, R. (2005). *A framework for understanding poverty*. Highlands, TX: Aha.

Pear, R. (2013, January 30). Federal rule limits aid to families who can't afford employers' health coverage. *New York Times*. Retrieved 9/25/13 from www.nytimes.com/2013/01/31/us/politics/irs-to-base-insurance-affordability-on-single-coverage.html

Pearson, P. D. (2013). Research foundations of the common core state standards in English language arts. In S. Neuamn & L. Gambrell (Eds.), *Quality reading instruction in the age of common core standards* (pp. 276–301). Newark: DE: International Reading Association.

Perez-Pena, R. (2012, May 30). Waivers for 8 more states from no child left behind. *New York Times*. Retrieved 9/25/13 from www.nytimes.com/2012/05/30/education/eight-more-states-get-waiver-from-no-child-law.html?_r=0

Peters, R.S. (1965). Education as initiation. In R. Archambault (Ed.), *Philosophical analysis and education* (pp. 87–111). New York: Routledge.

Petrosky, A. (2012, May 1). *Another perspective on close reading, the English/literacy common core state standards, and evidence based explanations*. Institute for Leadership. University of Pittsburgh. Retrieved 9/27/13 from http://ifl.lrdc.pitt.edu/ifl/index.php/blog/index/another_perspective_on_close_reading

References

Phillips, M. (2011). Parenting, time use and disparities in academic outcomes. In G. Duncan & R. Murnane (Eds.), *Whither opportunity? Rising inequality, schools, and children's life chances* (pp. 207–228). New York: Russell Sage Foundation.

President Obama's plan for early education for all Americans. (2013, February 13). White House factsheet. Retrieved 12/20/13 from www.whitehouse.gov/the-press-office/2013/02/13/fact-sheet-president-obama-s-plan-early-education-all-americans

Prospero. (2012, October 10). Class act. *The Economist*. Retrieved 9/23/13 from www.economist.com/blogs/prospero/2012/10/new-theatre-good-people

Ravitch, D. (1978). *The revisionists revised*. New York: Basic.

Ravitch, D. (1987). *The schools we deserve*. New York: Basic.

Ravitch, D. (1990/2000). *The American reader*. New York: William Morrow.

Ravitch, D. (2000). *Left back: A century of failed school reforms*. New York: Simon & Schuster.

Ravitch, D. (2004). *The language police*. New York: Vintage.

Ravitch, D. (2006). *The English reader*. New York: Oxford University.

Ravitch, D. (2007). *Ed speak*. Washington, DC: Association of Supervision & Curriculum Development.

Ravitch, D. (2010). *The death and life of the great American school system*. New York: Basic.

Reagan, R. (April 3, 1983). "A nation at risk" report. White House press release.

Reardon, S. (2011). The widening academic achievement gap between the rich and the poor. In G. Duncan & R. Murnane (Eds.), *Whither opportunity? Rising inequality, schools, and children's life chances* (pp. 91–116). New York: Russell Sage Foundation.

Rector, R., & Sheffield, R. (2011). Understanding poverty in the United States: Surprising facts about America's poor. *Backgrounder, 2607*. Heritage Foundation. Retrieved 9/24/13 from www.heritage.org/research/reports/2011/09/understanding-poverty-in-the-united-states-surprising-facts-about-americas-poor

Rich, M. (2013, August 15). School standards' debut is rocky, and critics pounce. *New York Times*. Retrieved 9/24/13 from www.nytimes.com/2013/08/16/education/new-education-standards-face-growing-opposition.html?pagewanted=all

Robelen, E. (2005, September 21). New Orleans eyed as a clean educational slate. *Education Week, 25*, 22–23. Retrieved 10/27/13 from www.edweek.org/ew/articles/2005/09/21/04katreform.h25.html

Robinson, K. (2010, October 14). *Changing education paradigm*. RSA animate. Retrieved 9/25/13 from www.youtube.com/watch?v=zDZFcDGpL4U

Rosenbaum, D. (2012, April 18). *Ryan budget would slash SNAP funding by $134 billion over ten years*. Center for Budget and Policy Priorities. Washington, DC. Retrieved 9/26/13 from www.cbpp.org/cms/index.cfm?fa=view&id=3717

Rothstein, R. (2004). *Class and schools*. New York: Teachers College.

Rousseau, J. J. (1762/1979). *Emile, or On education*. New York: Basic.

Rowan, B. (2011). Intervening to improve the educational outcomes of students in poverty. In G. Duncan & R. Murnane (Eds.), *Whither opportunity? Rising inequality, schools, and children's life chances* (pp. 523–538). New York: Russell Sage Foundation.

Sahlberg, P. (2011). *Finnish lessons: What can the world learn from educational change in Finland?* New York: Teachers College.

Sanchez, M. (May 21, 2013). Questions of accountability and fairness remain after charter school's reprieve. *Kansas City Star*. Retrieved 12/9/13 from www.google.com/url?sa=t&rct=j&q=&esrc=s&source=web&cd=1&ved=0CCsQFjAA&url=http%3A%2F%2Fwww.kansascity.com%2F2013%2F05%2F21%2F4248473%2Fquestions-of-accountability-and.html&ei=TS-mUrrJIPPMsQSzkIDwCA&usg=AFQjCNFH0rAfHcWQ1nPImvId983u1sMnIw&bvm=bv.57752919,d.cWc

References

Sastry, N., & Pebley, A. R. (2010). Family and neighborhood sources of socioeconomic inequality in children's achievement. *Demography, 47*(3), 777–800. Retrieved 9/27/13 from www.ncbi.nlm.nih.gov/pmc/articles/PMC3000065/

Schmitt, S. (2011, November). Early head start participants, programs, families and staff in 2011. CLASP. Washington, DC. Retrieved 9/26/13 from www.clasp.org/admin/site/publications/files/EHS-PIR-2011-Fact-Sheet.pdf

Secretariat. (2009). *Critical literacy.* CritSpecial Edition #9. Ontario Ministry of Education. Retrieved 9/24/13 from www.edu.gov.on.ca/eng/literacynumeracy/inspire/research/critical_literacy.pdf

Sedlak, A., Mettenburg, J., Basena, M., Petta, K., McPherson, K., Greene, A., & Li, S. (2010). The fourth national incidence study of child abuse and neglect. Report to Congress. Washington, DC: U.S. Department of Health and Human Services. Retrieved 9/25/13 from www.acf.hhs.gov/sites/default/files/opre/nis4_report_congress_full_pdf_jan2010.pdf

Shaefer, H., & Edin, K. (2012, February). *Extreme poverty in the United States, 1996 to 2011.* Policy Brief #28. National Poverty Center. University of Michigan. Retrieved 9/25/13 from www.npc.umich.edu/publications/policy_briefs/brief28/policybrief28.pdf

Shannon, P. (2007). *Reading against democracy: The broken promises of reading instruction.* Portsmouth, NH: Heinemann.

Shannon, P. (2011). *Reading wide awake: Politics, pedagogies & possibilities.* New York: Teachers College.

Sherman, A. (2011, November 7). *Poverty and financial distress would have been substantially worse in 2010 without government action.* Center on Budget and Policy Priorities. Retrieved 9/24/13 from www.cbpp.org/cms/?fa=view&id=3610

Sherman, A., Greenstein, R., & Ruffing, K. (2012, February 10). *Contrary to "entitlement society" rhetoric, over nine-tenths of entitlement benefits go to elderly, disabled, and working households.* Center on Budget and Policy Priorities. Retrieved 9/24/13 from www.cbpp.org/cms/?fa=view&id=3677

Short, K. (2012, November). *The research supplemental poverty measure*: 2011. Current Population Reports. The United States Census Bureau. Retrieved 9/25/13 from www.census.gov/prod/2012pubs/p60-244.pdf

Simon, W. (1978). *A time for truth.* New York: McGraw Hill.

Skinner, C. (2012, April). *Protecting the safety net in tough times.* National Center for Children in Poverty, Columbia University, New York. Retrieved 9/24/13 from www.nccp.org/publications/pdf/text_1061.pdf

Smith, A. (1776). *Inquiry into the nature and causes of the wealth of nations.* Retrieved 9/25/13 from www2.hn.psu.edu/faculty/jmanis/adam-smith/wealth-nations.pdf

Snow, C. (2002). *Reading for understanding: Toward an R & D program in reading comprehension.* RAND Corporation. Retrieved 9/25/13 from www.rand.org/content/dam/rand/pubs/monograph_reports/2005/MR1465.pdf

Snow, C., Burns, M., & Griffin, P. (1998). *Preventing reading difficulties in young children.* Washington, DC: National Academy Press.

Song, M., & Miskel, C. (2005). Who are the influential? A cross-state social network analysis of the reading policy domain. *Education Administration Quarterly, 41,* 7–48.

Street, B. (2012). Society reschooling. *Reading Research Quarterly, 47,* 216–227.

Taylor, D., & Dorsey-Gaines, C. (1988). *Growing up literate: Learning from inner city families.* Portsmouth, NH: Heinemann.

Teachout, T. (2011, March 4). Lindsay-Abaire's Southie class portrait. *Wall Street Journal.* Retrieved 9/23/13 from http://online.wsj.com/article/SB10001424052748704615504576172492540407986.html

References

Thompson, W., & Hickey, J. (2004). *Society in focus.* Boston, MA: Pearson.

Thorndike, E. L. (1906). *The principles of teaching based on psychology.* New York: A. G. Seeler.

Trimbur, J. (1992). Consensus and difference in collaborative learning. In P. Shannon (Ed.), *Becoming political.* Portsmouth, NH: Heinemann.

Tritch, T. (2011, November 19). Reading between the poverty lines. *New York Times.* Retrieved 9/24/13 from www.nytimes.com/2011/11/20/opinion/sunday/reading-between-the-poverty-lines.html

Ujufusa, A. (2012, November 19). Scores drop on Kentucky's common core-aligned tests. *Education Week.* Retrieved 9/24/13 from www.edweek.org/ew/articles/2012/11/02/11standards.h32.html

U.S. Census Bureau. (2011a, March). *Dynamics of economic well-being 2004–2006.* Retrieved 9/26/13 from www.census.gov/prod/2011pubs/p70–123.pdf

U.S. Census Bureau. (2011b). *Poverty.* Retrieved 9/26/13 from www.census.gov/hhes/www/poverty/data/threshld/

U.S. Census Bureau. (2012, September 12). *Income, poverty and health insurance coverage in the United States: 2011.* Retrieved 9/24/13 from www.census.gov/newsroom/releases/archives/income_wealth/cb12-172.html

Vasquez, V. (2004). *Negotiating critical literacies with young children.* Mahwah, NJ: Lawrence Erlbaum.

Waldfogel, J. (2009). The role of family policies in antipoverty policy. *Focus, 26,* 50–55. Retrieved 9/26/13 from www.irp.wisc.edu/publications/focus/pdfs/foc262i.pdf

Wallace, H. (1953, May 1). Liberalism reappraised. Speech at Harvard University. As quoted in J. Culver, *American dreamer* (2001). New York: Norton.

Wheaton, L., Giannarellie, L., Martinez-Schiferl, M., & Zedlewski, S. (2011, September). How do states' safety net policies affect poverty? *Working Families Paper 19.* The Urban Institute. Retrieved 9/24/13 from www.urban.org/uploadedpdf/412398-How-Do-State-Safety-Net-Policies-Affect-Poverty.pdf

Whitehurst, G. (2009, October). Don't forget the curriculum. *Brown Center Letters on Education #3.* Brookings Institute. Retrieved 9/25/13 from www.brookings.edu/research/papers/2009/10/14-curriculum-whitehurst

Whitehurst, G. (2013, January 23). Can we be hard headed about preschool? A look at universal and targeted pre-k. *The Brown Center Chalkboard.* Brookings Institute. Retrieved 9/24/13 from www.brookings.edu/blogs/brown-center-chalkboard/posts/2013/01/23-prek-whitehurst

Wight, V., Thampi, K., & Briggs, J. (2010). *Who are America's poor children? Examining food insecurity among children in the United States.* National Center for Children in Poverty. Columbia University, New York. Retrieved 9/25/13 from www.nokidhungry.org/sites/default/files/text_958.pdf

Wilkerson, R., & Pickett, K. (2009). *The spirit level: Why greater equality makes societies stronger.* New York: Bloomsbury.

Winship, S. (2011, November 9). Mobility impaired. *Social Genome Project Research #21.* Brookings Institute. Retrieved 9/25/13 from www.brookings.edu/research/articles/2011/11/09-economic-mobility-winship

Wise, E., & Long, D. (2013, April 22). *Market oriented education reforms' rhetoric trumps reality.* Broader Bolder Approach to Education. New York. Retrieved 9/27/13 from www.epi.org/files/2013/bba-rhetoric-trumps-reality.pdf

Wixson, K. (2012). Assessment and instruction in the era of the common core state standards in English language arts. Text Project. National Center for Literacy Education.

National Council of Teachers of English. Retrieved 9/25/13 from www.youtube.com/watch?v=vtk4f7UCns0

World Bank. (2013). Remarkable declines in global poverty, but major challenges remain. State of the Poor report. Retrieved 9/26/13 from www.worldbank.org/en/news/press-release/2013/04/17/remarkable-declines-in-global-poverty-but-major-challenges-remain

Yapa, L. (1996). What causes poverty?: A postmodern view. *Annals of the Association of American Geographers, 86,* 707–728.

INDEX

Note: Page numbers in *italics* indicate figures and tables.

absolute measure of poverty 14
access to health care 26
Achieve (nongovernmental agency) 87
Adams, Richard 102, 103, 106, 107
Adler, Mortimer 66
Adventures from the Book of Virtues (television series) 62
Affordable Care Act of 2010 21, 22
age and poverty 17
Anderson, Richard 41
antipoverty programs 4–5, 39; *see also* War on Poverty
Au, Kathryn 41–2, 51
Avila, JuliAnna 119–20

basic skills 75–6
BBA (Broader, Bolder Approach to Education) 39–40
Bell, Terrell 70, 72
Bennett, William 37, 60–3, 64, 70
Blanco, Kathleen 94
Bloom, A. 65–6
The Book of Virtues (Bennett) 60–3
Brantley, Ben 102, 103, 105, 107
Broader, Bolder Approach to Education (BBA) 39–40
Brooks, D. 58, 59
Bryk, Anthony 37–9, 51
Buckley, William F. 56, 67

Burke, Carolyn 41
Bush (G.H.W.) Administration 76
Bush (G.W.) Administration 51, 76

Calfee, Robert 89
Carolina Abecedarian Project 84
Celano, Donna 33–5, 36–7, 51, 63
Center for Inquiry 113–14
Center for Research on Education Outcomes (CREDO) 94–5
Chall, Jeanne S. 40
charter schools 93–5
Chicago School Reform Act of 1988 37–8
Child and Dependent Care Tax Credit 23
child-centered approach 68–9
Child Health Insurance Programs (CHIP) 22
children: poverty rates for 1, 17; safety net for 21–5, 42–3; school performance of 25–9
Child Tax Credit 23
citizenship, exclusions from 7–8
class: categorizations of 11–12; connotations of 9–10; economic mobility and 18; *Good People* and 101–3; preparation for school and 52
classrooms, liberal reading education in 40–2
Clinton, Bill x, 96
coalitions formed around social issues 5, 6
Coleman, David 87, 88, 100

Collaboration for Poverty Research (CPR) 28–9, 32
Commerce Clause 19
common core standards: four resources model and 120; liberal embrace of 51–2; neoliberals and 92–3, 97–9; Obama Administration and viii; overview of 86–90
community: liberal reading education in 33–7; radical democratic view of 109–11
compensatory reading education policy 46–53
competition in schooling 9–10, 93
concentrated poverty 17, 27
conservative position on poverty 3–4, 55–7, 77, 108
conservative reading education: after *A Nation at Risk* 74–7; becoming educated persons 64–8; books of virtue 60–3; in family 58–60; *A Nation at Risk* 71–4; policy 68–77; in schools 63–4
Council of Chief State School Officers (CCSSO) 87, 97
CREDO (Center for Research on Education Outcomes) 94–5
Cuban, Larry 43, 119

definitions of poverty: debate over 13–15; demographics and 16–19; "global poverty" 11; ideology and 12; Kristof and 3; "near poor" 11–12; Supplemental Poverty Measure and 15–16, *16*; thresholds *14*
democracy: ideological socialization and 6–8; reading and writing as recursive political acts in 103
disadvantage in schooling 9–10, 25–9
Duncan, Arne viii, 97
duration of poverty 17–18

Early Head Start 25
Earned Income Tax Credit (EITC) 21, 23
economic mobility 18
Edelman, Peter 4
educated person, becoming 64–8
EITC (Earned Income Tax Credit) 21, 23
elderly, poverty rates for 1, 3, 17
Elementary and Secondary Education Act (ESEA) of 1965: compensatory instruction 46–7; 50th anniversary of vii; liberal perspective 43–5; No Child Left Behind 47–53, 75, 76; purpose of 43; rationales for 35–6; Reagan Administration and 71; reauthorization of x–xi; Ryan budget and xi; Title 1 of 43–5
elementary education, radical democratic view of 113–14
An Elusive Science (Lagemann) 42
entitlement programs 19
ESEA *see* Elementary and Secondary Education Act (ESEA) of 1965
ethnicity and poverty 16–17

family and conservative reading education 58–60
federal assistance programs: for children 21–5, 42–3; financial eligibility for 14; overview of 19–21
financial eligibility for federal assistance programs 14, 19
food insecurity 26
four resources model of reading 116–18, 119, 120
Freebody, Peter 116–17
Friedman, Thomas, "So Much Fun. So Irrelevant" 79–81
fundamental attribution error 33

Gates, Bill 93, 98, 99, 120
gender and poverty 16
General Welfare Clause 19
Giving Our Children a Fighting Chance (Neuman and Celano) 33–5
"global poverty" 11
Goodman, Kenneth 41
Good People (Lindsay-Abaire): justice through participatory parity in 107–8; overview of 101–4; recognition in 105–6; redistribution in 104–5; representation in 106–7; solutions to poverty in 108–11
Gray, William S. 40
Great Books approach 65–6
Great Books Foundation 66
Great Recession 20–1, 24

Harlem on Our Minds (Kinloch) 114–16
Harste, Jerome 41
Hartman, Latoya 115
Hayek, Friedrich 56
Head Start program: Brooks on 59; Kristof and 3, 4; outcomes of 83, 84; overview of 20, 24–5; rationale for 35–6
health care, access to 26
Heath, Shirley Brice 36
Herrnstein, R. 59–60

Hess, Frederick 85–6, 99
Hiebert, Elfrieda 89
Highlander Research and Education Center 110, 111
high school education, radical democratic view of 114–16
high-stakes testing 76
Hill, Paul 94
Horton, Myles 110
housing: inadequate 26; public 22–3
Howe, Harold 45
Huey, Edmund Burke 40
Hurley, Rodger 35–6
Hutchins, Robert Mayer 66

ideological socialization and democracy 6–8
ideology and definitions of poverty 12
income distribution *10,* 10–11, 15–16, *16*
inequality 10–11, 28–9
informational capital 35, 52
in-school interventions: knowledge of ix; Race to the Top 97, 120; Reading First Initiative 49–50, 116; supports for change 38–9; *see also* common core standards; reading education
International Reading Association (IRA) 46
international test scores viii–ix, 118–19
"It Works" project 45

Johnson Administration vii, 24–5, 43
justice through participatory parity 104, 107–8, 121–2

Kaufman, Greg 110
Kay, Ken 90
Kennedy, John 31, 32
Kennedy, Robert 43–4
Kentucky: culture of poverty in 1; Save the Children program in 3
Keppel, Francis vii, 44
Kinloch, Valerie 114–16
Knowledge Is Power Program (KIPP) 96
Kristof, Nicholas D., "Profiting from a Child's Illiteracy" 1–5, 59
Kristol, William 57, 67

Lagemann, Ellen Condliffe 42
liberal democratic theory 28, 31–3
liberal position on poverty 3, 32, 53, 107
liberal reading education: in classrooms 40–2; in community 33–7; policy 42–53; in schools 37–40
libraries, income and uses of 33–5

Lincoln, Abraham 61–2
Lindsay-Abaire, David 101–4; *see also Good People*
Loveless, Tom 98
low birth weight 26
Luke, Allan 116–17

market orientation to education 76–7, 84–5
Medicaid 21
Moats, Louisa 41–2
Moore, Michael 120
Murray, Charles: *The Bell Curve* 59–60; *Coming Apart* vii, x, 60; on Head Start 59; *Losing Ground* 59; views of on education 67

National Assessment of Educational Progress (NAEP) 50, 51, 84
National Commission on Excellence in Education (NCEE) 71–4, 75, 76, 77
National Education Association 68, 70, 73, 90
National Governors Association (NGA) 86–7, 92, 97
National Institute for Early Education Research 52
National Reading Panel (NRP) 48–9, 50, 51
National School Lunch Program 22
A Nation at Risk 71–4, 75, 76
NCEE (National Commission on Excellence in Education) 71–4, 75, 76, 77
NCLB (No Child Left Behind) Act of 2001 47–53, 75, 76, 116
"near poor" 11–12
Negotiating Critical Literacies with Young Children (Vasquez) 112–13
neoliberal position: overview of 79–81; on poverty 4, 81–2, 99, 108
neoliberal reading education: policy 92–100; 21st-century 85–92; universal preschool 82–5
Neuman, Susan 33–5, 36–7, 51, 63
New Orleans, charter schools in 94
New South Wales, Australia 117–18
NGA (National Governors Association) 86–7, 92, 97
No Child Left Behind (NCLB) Act of 2001 47–53, 75, 76, 116
No Excuses schools 96–7
NRP (National Reading Panel) 48–9, 50, 51

Obama, Barack: agenda of x–xi; on charter schools 95; on Common Core State

Standards 92; on education vii; educational reform and 82–3; on universal preschool 25
O'Keefe, Timothy 113, 114
Ontario Language Curriculum 118
out-of-school supports: antipoverty programs 4–5, 39; Broader, Bolder Approach to Education 39–40; overview of ix; *see also* federal assistance programs

parents and conservative reading education 58–60
Partnership for 21st Century Skills (P21) 90–2
paternalistic schooling 36–7, 39, 63
Pearson, P. David 89, 120
performance gap in test scores viii–ix
Perry School Project 84
Peters, R. S. 64, 67
Petrosky, Anthony 89
Pinker, Steven 31, 32
Planning, Programming, and Budgeting System (PPBS) of ESEA 44–5, 47
poverty: consequences of 3, 9–12, 25–9; conservative position on 3–4, 56–7, 77, 108; liberal position on 3, 32, 53, 107; as national disgrace 1–8; neoliberal position on 4, 81–2, 99, 108; radical democratic position on 104–8; *see also* definitions of poverty
Poverty and Mental Retardation (Hurley) 35–6
power relations and poverty 6–8, 28–9, 107
PPBS (Planning, Programming, and Budgeting System) of ESEA 44–5, 47
Pratt, Carolyn 40
preschool programs: radical democratic view of 112–13; support for 52–3, 59; universal 25, 82–5; *see also* Head Start program
professional organizations, influence of x
Progress in International Reading Literacy Study xiii
Project Follow Through 45
Prospero 102, 103
public housing 22–3
public schooling: competition in 9–10; neoliberal position on 85–92; outcomes of vii–viii

race and poverty 16–17
Race to the Top 97, 120

radical democrats: overview of 101–4; reading education 111–16; reading education policy 116–22; solutions to poverty 108–11; view of poverty 104–8
Ravitch, Diane: common core standards and 89; critiques by 65, 69; on favorite English teacher 67; *Left Back* 68; on NCEE recommendations 74, 77
reading: ideologies and forms of 7–8; as recursive political act 103; *see also* reading education; reading education policy
reading education: conservative approach to 58–68; liberal approach to 33–42; neoliberal approach to 82–92; radical Democratic approach to 111–16
reading education policy: conservative approach to 68–77; liberal approach to 42–53; neoliberal approach to 92–100; radical Democratic approach to 116–22
Reading First Implementation Study 50–1
Reading First Initiative 49–50, 116
Reagan, Ronald 57, 70–1, 73–4
recognition 104, 105–6
redistribution 104–5
regional poverty 17
Reich, Robert 122
representation 104, 106–7
Robinson, Ken 85
Romney, Mitt xi, 12
Rousseau, J. J. 68
Ryan, Paul: "Paths to Prosperity" budget vii, x; as vice-presidential candidate xi

Save the Children program 3
school performance, consequences of poverty on 25–9
schools, reading education in: conservative 63–4; liberal 37–42; neoliberal 95–100; radical democratic 111–16
scientific management 68–9
scientific rationality 40–2
The Sharon Statement 55–6
Simon, William 57
Smith, Adam 28
SNAP (Supplemental Nutritional Assistance Program) 19, 22, 24, 42–3
social benefits: federal assistance programs 14, 19–21; perceptions of 12
social safety net: for children 21–5, 42–3; overview of 19–21
Social Security 19–20
sociological imaginations 5, 6

SPM (Supplemental Poverty Measure) 15–16, *16*
SSI (Supplemental Security Income) program 1
standards 75; *see also* common core standards
Street, Brian 116
Supplemental Nutritional Assistance Program (SNAP) 19, 22, 24, 42–3
Supplemental Poverty Measure (SPM) 15–16, *16*
Supplemental Security Income (SSI) program 1

teachers: conservative education policy and 74; dispositions of 95–7
Teach for America 95–6
Teachout, Terry 102, 103, 105, 107
TEMPO evaluation 44–5
Temporary Assistance for Needy Families (TANF) 24
temporary poverty 17–18
Tennessee, Race to the Top in 97
test scores: Common Core and 120; improving ix; international viii–ix, 118–19

Thorndike, E. L. 69
toxic stress 26–7

unemployment insurance 24
Urban Academy 36
U.S. Census Bureau Supplemental Poverty Measure (SPM) 15–16, *16*

Van Sluys, Katie 89
Vasquez, Vivian 112–13
virtues and conservative reading education 60–2

wage gaps 16, 17
Wallace, Henry A. 31, 32
War on Poverty vii, 24–5, 43
Ways With Words (Heath) 36
Whitehurst, G. 84–5
Wider Opportunities for Women (WOW) 14–15
Witnesses to Hunger programs 110–11
Wixson, Karen 89
Woodward, Virginia 41
writing, as recursive political act 103

YES Prep 96–7